On CLO
READING

T0268823

On CLOSE READING

John Guillory

WITH AN ANNOTATED
BIBLIOGRAPHY BY
Scott Newstok

THE UNIVERSITY OF CHICAGO PRESS
Chicago and London

The University of Chicago Press, Chicago 60637
The University of Chicago Press, Ltd., London
© 2025 by The University of Chicago
All rights reserved. No part of this book may be used or
reproduced in any manner whatsoever without written
permission, except in the case of brief quotations in critical articles
and reviews. For more information, contact the University of
Chicago Press, 1427 East 60th Street, Chicago, IL 60637.
Published 2025
Printed in the United States of America

34 33 32 31 30 29 28 27 26 25   1 2 3 4 5

ISBN-13: 978-0-226-83742-0 (cloth)
ISBN-13: 978-0-226-83743-7 (paper)
ISBN-13: 978-0-226-83744-4 (e-book)
DOI: https://doi.org/10.7208/chicago/9780226837444.001.0001

Library of Congress Cataloging-in-Publication Data

Names: Guillory, John, author. | Newstok, Scott L., 1973–
Title: On close reading / John Guillory ; with an annotated
    bibliography by Scott Newstok.
Description: Chicago : The University of Chicago Press, 2025. |
    Includes bibliographical references and index.
Identifiers: LCCN 2024017544 | ISBN 9780226837420 (cloth) |
    ISBN 9780226837437 (paperback) | ISBN 9780226837444 (ebook)
Subjects: LCSH: Close reading. | Criticism.
Classification: LCC PN98.C57 G85 2025 | DDC 428.4—dc23/eng/20240525
LC record available at https://lccn.loc.gov/2024017544

♾ This paper meets the requirements of ANSI/NISO Z39.48-1992
(Permanence of Paper).

CONTENTS

PREFACE

This small book aims to solve two large puzzles in the history of Anglo-American literary criticism. The first is the question of why the term "close reading" was so infrequently invoked in the decades after its initial mention in I. A. Richards's *Practical Criticism*. In fact, the term did not achieve consensus recognition in literary studies until the later 1950s, on the threshold of New Criticism's decline.

The second puzzle concerns the inability of scholars to define the procedure of close reading in any but the most uncertain terms, usually not much more than is implied by the spatial figure "close." Sometimes this figure is elucidated by the notion of reading with "attention to the words on the page." Yet it does not take much research to establish that reading with attention to the words on the page characterizes many practices of reading from antiquity to the present. How can "close reading" name a practice of such scope and duration and yet be seen as emergent during the interwar period of the twentieth century?

These two puzzles are intertwined. The premise of my argument is that the literary critics of the interwar period—both the representatives of "practical criticism" and the American New Critics—were not aiming at first to devise a method of reading at all. Following the lead of T. S. Eliot, these critics—I. A. Richards, F. R. Leavis, Cleanth Brooks, W. K. Wimsatt, and their peers—were most urgently concerned to establish the *judgment of literature* on more rigorous grounds than had previously obtained in criticism. In the course of forming a conception of literature that would function as the basis for judgment, they developed a corollary *technique of reading* that confirmed the value of the literary work of art in a universe of new media and mass forms of writing. This technique initially had no name, although it was soon recognized by contemporaries as something new, different from the procedure of the literary historians who dominated the language and literature departments at the time. Our recollection today of the technique's importance as a methodological innovation suppresses its context in the problem of judgment—or rather, forgets this context. We look back on this moment in the history of the discipline and wonder why the literary critics of the time did not recognize what seems to us now their major achievement.

The marginality of the term "close reading" during the decades after its appearance in Richards's *Practical Criticism* was correlated to the difficulty critics had in defining their new practice of reading as a precise sequence of actions. The absence of a definite procedure for close reading contrasts strikingly with the rich aesthetic vocabulary of the New Critics—their development of notions of cultural sensibility (as found in Leavis) and of an "ontology" of the literary work of art (as seen in Brooks, John Crowe Ransom, and René Wellek). It is my contention that the difficulty of defining close reading is an entailment of its nature *as technique*. Or more precisely, as *cultural technique*, a very particular kind of methodical human action. All cultural techniques resist definition of the sort that specifies the sequence and components of methodical action. Techniques must be understood as inclusive of the most universal and mundane activities, even the most basic bodily techniques, such as swimming, dancing, riding a bicycle, even tying shoelaces. These cultural techniques can be described, and they can be taught, but they cannot be specified verbally in such a way as to permit their transmission by verbal means alone. Techniques are transmitted rather by *demonstration* and *imitation*. The fact of their resistance to precise definition does not contradict their complexity as human actions. Techniques can be described in minimal terms, but they are not necessarily simple. No cultural technique exhibits this paradoxical aspect more than reading, the genus of human action to which close reading belongs as a species, a specialization.

At the core of literary study, then, is a technique with a history, but no precise verbal formula for performance. The technique of close reading can be *described* but not *prescribed*. By means of this technique, literary study established its identity as a discipline, despite efforts to repudiate the technique early in its history as mechanical or pseudoscientific, and later to reject it as mired in the social and ideological conditions of its emergence. The history of Anglo-American literary study records the long effort of scholars to come to terms with the muteness of their discipline's core technique.

In giving an account of this history, I have had occasion to reflect on the question: What is a "technical" term? Literary study is replete with such terms, but for some reason, "close reading" has for the most part fallen out of the discipline's technical lexicon. The concept of "technique," which I draw from the work of anthropologists such as Marcel Mauss and employ as a means of understanding modes of reading as transmissible human actions, offers a way forward with this problem. Close reading, as a technique *without concept* (to invoke Kant's analogous effort to understand aesthetic perception), constitutes the infrastructure for all disciplinary modes of interpretation, from the formalism of the New Critics to deconstruction, New Historicism, and even, I will argue, what has come to be known as "distant reading." Finally, I aim to bring the technique of close reading into relation to the long history of writing and reading as cultural techniques, among the most important techniques in the history of human culture, perhaps exceeded only by the gift of Prometheus.

On CLOSE READING

This construing, we must suppose, is not nearly so easy and "natural" a performance as we tend to assume. It is a craft, in the sense that mathematics, cooking, and shoe-making are crafts. It can be taught.

I. A. RICHARDS, *Practical Criticism: A Study of Literary Judgment* (1929)

In spite of the ugly associations attached to such terms as method and analysis the responsible critic is obliged to give an account of what he is doing, of how he works. He will not succeed, of course, since no one, including the technologist, ever describes exactly what he does. However conscious the operator may be, there is always some point at which he becomes inarticulate; some indispensable act of perception, of co-ordination of eye and hand, always lies beyond expression.

REUBEN ARTHUR BROWER, *The Fields of Light: An Experiment in Critical Reading* (1951)

THE RISE AND RISE OF
CLOSE READING

The term "close reading," which for decades was largely absent from literary theory, has reemerged in recent years as the subject of wide discussion. Why has close reading returned to the forefront of criticism?[1] Why does it name an antagonist to be vanquished again, after what seemed to be its permanent demotion in the era of New Historicism? Conversely, why has close reading attracted so many efforts of late to reaffirm its importance in literary criticism, even as the core practice of the discipline? In either case, the notion of close reading is clearly unfinished business for literary study.[2]

1. Throughout this book, I use quotation marks to refer to "close reading" as a term, omitting the quotation marks when I refer to the practice.

2. The scholarship on close reading is too voluminous to permit more than a sampling in these notes. The resurgence of interest in close reading began in the later 1990s and continues into the present, sometimes, though not always, in response to the emergence of "distant reading." For an early statement, see Douglas Mao, "The New Critics and the Text Object," *ELH* 61.1 (Spring 1996): 227–254. Scholarship attesting to a shift in the valuation of close reading includes: *Close Reading: The Reader*, ed. Andrew DuBois and Frank Lentricchia (Durham, NC: Duke University Press, 2003); Isobel Armstrong, "Textual Harassment: The Ideology of Close Reading, or How Close Is Close?," in *The Radical Aesthetic* (Oxford: Blackwell, 2000), 85–107; Jane Gallop, "The Historicization of Literary Studies and the Fate of Close Reading," *Profession* (2007): 181–186; Jonathan Culler, "The Closeness of Close Reading," *ADE Bulletin* 149 (2010): 20–25; Jane Gallop, "Close Reading in 2009," *ADE Bulletin* 149 (2010): 15–19; John Guillory, "Close Reading: Prologue and Epilogue," *ADE Bulletin* 149 (2010): 8–14; N. Katherine Hayles, "How We Read: Close, Hyper, Machine," *ADE Bulletin* 150 (2010): 62–79; *Rereading the New Criticism*, ed. Miranda B. Hickman and John D. McIntyre (Columbus: Ohio State University Press, 2012); Helen Thaventhiran, *Radical Empiricists: Five Modernist Close Readers*

It is widely assumed that "close reading" was a term of art for the New Criticism, but the historical record does not support this belief. One searches in vain for evidence in the 1930s and 1940s that "close reading" was a common expression among the New Critics, an absence so remarkable as to raise the possibility that this practice had only a phantom existence. Returning to I. A. Richards, who is sometimes said to be the inventor of close reading, we find in his landmark *Practical Criticism* of 1929 several instances of "close," "closer," and "closely" as qualifiers of "reading," including what seems in retrospect like an acknowledgment of the practice itself: "All respectable poetry invites close reading."[3] Yet Richards does not go on in this passage, or anywhere else in his book, to describe a procedure of close reading more precise than is already indicated by the spatial trope. It is not at all obvious what "close" entails in reading a poem. In fact, *Practical Criticism* is devoid of any demonstration of close reading in the manner that would later acquire this name.

(Oxford: Oxford University Press, 2015); Barbara Herrnstein Smith, "What Was 'Close Reading': A Century of Method in Literary Studies," *the minnesota review* 87 (2016): 57–75; Jay Jin, "Problems of Scale in 'Close' and 'Distant' Reading," *Philological Quarterly* 96.1 (Winter 2017): 105–129; *Modernism and Close Reading*, ed. David James (Oxford: Oxford University Press, 2020). For an overview, see Angus Connell Brown, "Between Lines: Close Reading, Quotation, and Critical Style from Practical Criticism to Queer Theory" (PhD thesis, Oxford University, 2014). Since Brown's work, comment on close reading has swelled into dozens of essays and many hundreds of citations, a development that one might not have predicted only a decade before that. For additional bibliography, see Scott Newstok, "Annotated Bibliography," and online "Archive."

3. I. A. Richards, *Practical Criticism: A Study of Literary Judgment* (San Diego, CA: Harcourt Brace, 1929), 195. Richards does not invoke "close reading" in his publications of the next several decades.

Richards is rather concerned to explore the problem of *mis-reading*, the interferences that undermine the very possibility of comprehending a poem.

Linking the descriptor "close" to the word "reading" is no more surprising or unusual than linking it to other action verbs or nouns, as in the phrase "to pay close attention." In the absence of a given context, "close reading" suggests little more than reading a piece of writing with enhanced care or attention. I will refer to this more general sense by the phrase, "reading closely," which would include all instances of careful or methodical reading, whatever the aim or context of that reading. Instances of reading closely in this more capacious sense are legion and include the long history of biblical commentary as well as the philological and textual criticism that emerged during the Renaissance.[4] Because the term "close reading" has not acquired a consensus definition in literary study, some scholars want to equate the term with any attentive practice of reading. Michael Hancher, for example, argues that all uses of the term "close reading," whatever their time or place, refer to the same procedure.[5] Although I believe that this is a mistaken generalization, Hancher's argument suggests why the terminological problem has been so intractable. The low information content of the qualifier "close" (however suggestive as a trope) is one reason why the new reading technique of the interwar period could be

4. There was once a single English word for this sense of reading closely— "perusal"—which at the time of its introduction into English in the sixteenth century meant any careful examination of a piece of writing. In the later nineteenth century, the meaning of this word surprisingly flipped over into the opposite sense of a casual mode of reading.

5. Michael Hancher, "Re: Search and Close Reading," *Debates in the Digital Humanities 2016* (Minneapolis: University of Minnesota Press, 2016), 118–138.

disseminated without fixing exclusively on the name of "close reading." Other terms could and did serve the purpose of gesturing toward this technique of reading, such as "explication," "exegesis," and "verbal analysis." It took several decades for "close reading" to crowd out its competitors, that is, for the bigram to provoke an immediate association among the literary professoriate with a technique of reading descending from the New Critics. This history of semantic uncertainty is difficult for us even to recall today, because the term "close reading" has for many years been locked into a disciplinary matrix of circulation.[6]

For two decades after Richards's *Practical Criticism*, use of the term "close reading" was relatively uncommon in the writing of literary critics, including the New Critics. It is conspicuously absent from the work of William Empson, F. R. Leavis, Cleanth Brooks, W. K. Wimsatt, and other prominent critics in the decade after *Practical Criticism*. It is nowhere to be found in the indexes to the major works of the New Critics in this period. One exception is Stanley Edgar Hyman's 1948 survey of the critical field, *The Armed Vision*. Hyman is not a New Critic, but he uses forms of the adjective "close" to describe the practice of some contemporary critics, such as R. P. Blackmur, "the sharpest and closest reader of poetry we have," and William Empson, whose *Seven Types of Ambiguity* is praised as "the finest close reading of poetry

---

6. This point is clearly and correctly stated by Andrew DuBois, "Close Reading: An Introduction," in Frank Lentricchia and Andrew DuBois, eds., *Close Reading: The Reader* (Durham, NC: Duke University Press, 2003): "As a term, *close reading* hardly seems to leave the realm of so-called common sense, where it would appear to mean something understandable and vague like 'reading with special attention'; but it is also jargon, albeit jargon of a not uninviting variety" (2).

ever put down."[7] Hyman is not quite invoking a term of art, as his discussion of Cleanth Brooks and Robert Penn Warren's *Understanding Poetry* confirms. Summing up the aims of this work, he writes that it "sponsors a certain amount of close reading and structural analysis as well as Brooks's 'tradition'" (94). In the decade before Hyman was writing, the New Critics' revisionist literary history, a legacy of T. S. Eliot's criticism, might well have made a greater impression on scholars than their technique of reading, especially as their as yet unbaptized mode of reading was associated in those early years more with teaching than with scholarship. If *Understanding Poetry* came to be regarded as the bible of close reading, contemporary scholars were taking note of Brooks's elevation of Donne and the metaphysicals as model poets, inaugurating a revaluation of the entire poetic tradition.

Writing in the same year as Hyman, René Wellek and Austin Warren in *Theory of Literature* refer once in the body of their book to "close reading and exegesis."[8] The qualifier "close" seems to need the help of "exegesis" for clarification. They use the term more indexically, however, in section IV of their bibliography, titled "Discussions of 'Close Reading' and Examples of Methods" (328). The use of quotation marks hints that although the term was in circulation by the later 1940s, it was perhaps most common in conversation—what we would today call a meme.[9] The term is absent from

7. Stanley Edgar Hyman, *The Armed Vision: A Study of the Methods of Modern Literary Criticism* (New York: Alfred A. Knopf, 1948), 270, 277.

8. René Wellek and Austin Warren, *Theory of Literature* (New York: Harcourt Brace, 1948), 294.

9. In his survey of this terrain, Jin, "Problems of Scale," 107–111, finds some instances of the term "close reading" in discussions during the interwar period of literary education at the pre-college level. These instances are not, in my

William Elton's nearly contemporaneous 1949 volume, *A Glossary of the New Criticism*, although Elton does observe in his introduction that Cleanth Brooks and Robert Penn Warren have spread "the gospel of close textual analysis."[10] Again, a meme is implied. Also in 1949, Douglas Bush remarks in an otherwise severe critique of the New Critics that their preference for "close reading of poetry has braced the flaccid sinews of this generation of readers and has had some highly beneficial effects upon teaching and writing."[11] Bush uses the phrase only once in his essay; the context makes it clear that he is not referring to a precise term of art so much as characterizing a general tendency of New Critical practice, a preference for a mode of reading that looks different from the procedure of the literary historians.

If "close reading" circulated somewhat more frequently in print as the 1950s progressed, it remains difficult to find instances of its use by New Critics themselves. There is evidence, however, that a number of critics recognized the spread of the technique, especially those who entertained reservations. Here is a typical example from an essay by John

view, instances of the technique of reading developing in Practical Criticism and New Criticism, but they do express a shared anxiety about basic reading skills.

10. William Elton, *A Glossary of the New Criticism* (Chicago: Modern Poetry Association, 1948, 1949), 4. The tenuous status of "close reading" as a term in literary *theory*—it circulated rather as the name of a *practice*—persisted for many decades thereafter. Wendell V. Harris's excellent summary of literary theory, *Dictionary of Concepts in Literary Criticism and Theory* (New York: Greenwood Press, 1992), for example, still contains no independent entry on close reading, nor an index citation. Harris does, however, refer to "close reading" in his entry on New Criticism (270).

11. Douglas Bush, "The New Criticism: Some Old-Fashioned Queries," *PMLA* 64.1 (March 1949): 13.

Holloway, published in *The Hudson Review* of 1953: "The present argument, then, is that the lineage of 'close reading' as a critical method is impure; deriving in part from a keener sense of the distinctiveness of poetry, which was an asset; and in part from an excessive though perhaps half-conscious respect for science, which was a liability."[12] Other instances from the 1950s might be cited, but even in this decade, a golden age of interpretive criticism for literary study, the use of the term in print is less frequent than in later decades.[13] The problem, to underscore, is not the entire absence of the term "close reading" from critical discourse, but the fact that it was not—as we might expect from our contemporary vantage—ubiquitous. A decade after Holloway, René Wellek invokes it several times in his *Concepts of Criticism*. In that

12. John Holloway, "The Critical Intimidation," *The Hudson Review* 5.4 (Winter 1953): 474–495. I quote the passage from its republication in John Holloway, *The Charted Mirror: Literary and Critical Essays* (New York: Horizon Press, 1962), 171.

13. For other mentions of close reading in the early 1950s, see Clarence L. Kulishek, "The New Criticism and the New College Text," *Journal of Higher Education* 25.4 (April 1954): 173–178, 227–228. Significant mentions include Jacques Barzun, "The Scholar-Critic," in *Contemporary Literary Scholarship: A Critical Review*, ed. Lewis Leary (New York: Appleton-Century-Crofts, 1958): 7; and in the same volume, William Van O'Connor, "Modern Literary Criticism," 224. Often close reading is recognized as a controversial method, as in Monroe Beardsley, "Analysis," in Joseph T. Shipley, *Dictionary of World Literature: Criticism—Forms—Technique* (New York: Philosophical Library, 1953): "This sort of verbal analysis, or 'close reading', is constantly under attack from those who claim that it 'falsifies' literature, that it interferes with the unified intuitive understanding of poetry, and that it is sterile" (24). R. S. Crane acknowledges New Criticism as the competitor to the Aristotelianism of the Chicago School in the introduction to *Critics and Criticism: Ancient and Modern*, ed. R. S. Crane (Chicago: University of Chicago Press, 1952): "we must mention . . . the strong emphasis placed by academic representatives of the school [the New Critics] on the 'close reading' of texts" (15).

volume we find "close reading" again in quotation marks, but no one critic or text is cited as the origin of the term.[14] Wellek continues to put quotation marks around the term in his *Discriminations* of 1970, possibly because "close reading" is still being used more in conversation than in print.[15] The use of quotation marks sometimes continues into the present, confirming the humble origins of the term as a borrowing from ordinary usage.

The wider dissemination of "close reading" in the later 1960s and after coincided with the decline of the New Criticism. This coincidence suggests that a revisionist history of the New Criticism was implicated in literary study's effort to reinvent itself in the age of High Theory. Close reading seemed an ambiguous legacy, both a foundational practice for the discipline and a holdover from a supposedly pretheoretical era.[16] Although close textual analysis was common in scholarship of this period, by the later 1970s it was usually identified with versions of continental theory and carefully distinguished from New Critical doctrines, such as the

14. René Wellek, *Concepts of Criticism* (New Haven, CT: Yale University Press, 1963), 9. For Wellek, it needs something of an apology: "'Close reading' has led to pedantries and aberrations, as have all the other methods of scholarship; but it is surely here to stay" (9). He associates close reading particularly with Cleanth Brooks (7) and R. P. Blackmur (307). The chapter was originally published as "Literary Theory, Criticism, and History," *The Sewanee Review* 68.1 (Winter 1960): 1–19.

15. René Wellek, *Discriminations: Further Concepts of Criticism* (New Haven, CT: Yale University Press, 1970): 264.

16. A certain defensiveness about the term "close reading" is expressed in later decades even by Brooks himself. In "The New Criticism," *The Sewanee Review* 87.4 (Fall 1979): 592–607, Brooks seems reluctant to own the term, suggesting that another phrase, "adequate reading," would do just as well (600).

notion of "organic unity."[17] At the same time, what was called "close reading" was increasingly relegated to the introductory level of literary study.[18] With the advent of New Historicism, close reading was subjected to a more thoroughgoing, if largely implicit, critique in arguments against the residual "formalism" of High Theory.[19] Consulting Google Ngram (for what this sampling is worth), I note that the phrase "close reading" seems to have increased suddenly in frequency in the 1980s. For several decades following, from the end of the 1980s to the second decade of the new century, close reading was a practice less central to theory, if also quietly enduring

17. Specifying the relation between theory's version of reading and its New Critical predecessor was difficult, especially with deconstruction. On the one side, see Mary Jacobus, "Introduction," *Yale French Studies* 62 (1981): "deconstruction is exactly close reading" (11). On the other, see Lawrence I. Lipking, "The Practice of Theory," *Profession* (1983): "Most deconstructionists, to be sure, reject this association with close reading. They prefer to regard their enterprise not as a method but as the subversion of any method, not as close reading but as the detonation, primed from within, of any stable reading" (22).

18. See William Schaefer, "Editor's Column," *PMLA* 93.2 (March 1978): "In the forty years since Brooks and Warren published *Understanding Poetry*, explication de texte has become somewhat unfashionable, with 'close reading' now being left, for the most part, to the undergraduate and to those who create multiple-choice questions for college entrance examinations" (179). The identification of close reading with *explication de texte* is an error, but Schaefer's perception about the lower place of close reading in the curriculum is telling.

19. Newstok's "Archive" discloses little comment among the New Historicists on the subject of "close reading," but my recollection is that the central issue in theoretical debate shifted away from the question of reading, which was central to deconstruction in both the Derridean and the de Manian versions, to a supposed conflict between formalism and historicism. Close reading was hidden in the antagonist whose name was "formalism." But proof of this hypothesis would require further research. What does strike me as indisputable is that a conflict between historicism and formalism structured literary theory from the 1980s forward. Historicism increasingly prevailed in this conflict.

JOHN GUILLORY

as the mainstay of introductory literature courses. This was also the period during which it was possible to object strenuously to close reading's centrality in literary study, as in Peter Rabinowitz's blast in his well-known essay of 1992, "Against Close Reading": "close reading is neither the natural, nor necessarily the best way to approach a text."[20] Pronouncements such as these brought close reading only temporarily into disrepute. Since at least the second decade of the twenty-first century, close reading seems to have become the object of renewed interest, largely tending toward reaffirmation.

From the vantage of the present, it would appear that close reading has always been with us, at the center of our discipline. If close reading has been marginal in literary theory, it has been central to practice. The puzzle of its actual belatedness as a term of art raises a difficult historiographical problem. I suggest that this problem might be partially clarified by acknowledging a principle of *foreshortening* governing literary study's perception of its earlier history. Close reading looms large to later generations of scholars as the major achievement of New Criticism, its most powerful legacy; yet in its nascent form, it competed with many

20. Peter Rabinowitz, "Against Close Reading," in *Pedagogy is Politics: Literary Theory and Critical Teaching*, ed. Maria-Regina Kecht (Chicago: University of Illinois Press, 1992), 230–243. Such dismissals were common in the 1980s and 1990s, acknowledged by J. Hillis Miller, "Teaching *Middlemarch*: Close Reading and Theory," in *Approaches to Teaching Eliot's Middlemarch*, ed. Kathleen Blake (New York: MLA, 1991): "A good bit of hostility is expressed here and there these days to close reading" (51). By the end of the decade, some critics want to argue for its expulsion from the discipline. See Mary Poovey, "Beyond the Current Impasse in Literary Studies," *American Literary History* 11.2 (Summer 1999): "If formalist methods are to be discarded, then another method—equally capable of specifying a discipline— needs to replace close reading" (372).

other tendencies in academic literary study. In fact, theo-
retically minded critics of the interwar period were primar-
ily engaged in efforts to establish the judgment of literary
works on more rigorous grounds than those which formerly
prevailed in critical discourse. This was the great project of
T. S. Eliot, who, although not the inventor of close reading,
established some of the principles that enabled its development.[21] The revisionist history of English literature, already
remarked, was the result of a very ambitious theoretical effort, the construction of a new ontology of the literary artifact, correlated with a reconsideration of long-standing
judgments about individual writers. There is no question,
however, that a practice of reading also emerged at the end
of the 1920s that ultimately transformed the discipline of literary study.[22] It may be that the way in which we recollect
this event today says as much about recent developments in
the discipline as about the interwar period itself. The resurgence of interest in close reading in recent years is, I will

21. Chief among Eliot's innovations was his extensive use of quotation,
dedicated to exemplifying an evaluative proposition rather than an interpretive argument. See Geoffrey Hartman, *Criticism in the Wilderness: The Study
of Literature Today* (New Haven, CT: Yale University Press, 1980): "Eliot
quotes closely rather than reads closely" (175).

22. In this essay I do not identify any one critic or group of critics as the
inventors of close reading. For an argument of this sort, see Donald J. Childs,
*The Birth of the New Criticism: Conflict and Conciliation in the Early Work of
William Empson, I. A. Richards, Laura Riding, and Robert Graves* (Montreal:
McGill-Queen's University Press, 2013). Childs argues for the origin of New
Critical reading in the work of Laura Riding and Robert Graves, especially the
work that had a great impact on William Empson, *A Survey of Modernist Poetry* (London: William Heinemann, 1927). In my view, the influence of Riding
and Graves has been overemphasized by Childs and others, but my reasons for
this position are too complex to rehearse here.

suggest, connected to an ongoing legitimation crisis, a loss of faith in disciplinary modes of reading, which has given rise to calls for alternatives such as "postcritical" reading or "surface reading," as well as for the computational mode of analysis known as "distant reading."[23]

Correcting for the distortions of foreshortening as well as we are able, it is evident that close reading as a practice reached the zenith of its dominance in the period from the 1940s to the later 1960s. Although literary scholarship in those decades ceased to exhibit the ideological investments of the New Criticism—the reactionary political movement known as Southern Agrarianism, along with the tacit profession of Anglo-Catholicism—it continued to manifest certain familiar New Critical features, such as an orientation to passages of text seen as ambiguous, or marked by the conspicuous use of figurative language. These features, among others, constituted a loose collection of foci for disciplinary reading.

23. For two major statements, see Rita Felski, *The Limits of Critique* (Chicago: University of Chicago Press, 2015); and Stephen Best and Sharon Marcus, "Surface Reading: An Introduction," *Representations* 108.1 (Fall 2009): 1–21. (For a discussion of these and related arguments, see *Professing Criticism: Essays on the Organization of Literary Study* [Chicago: University of Chicago Press, 2022], 83–102.) Something that might be called "reading studies" seems to be emerging at this moment. Not just a subfield of book history, reading studies would incorporate book history into a larger interdisciplinary inquiry with sites in social history, literary study, digital analysis, affect studies, and the neurophysiology of reading, the latter discussed further below. For an inaugural survey, see *Further Reading*, ed. Matthew Rubery and Leah Price (Oxford: Oxford University Press, 2020). The editors of this volume invoke close reading in the background of the essays collected in the volume, noting: "Intensive critical analysis is now merely one methodology among many as literary critics continue spinning out taxonomies of reading styles: deep, descriptive, denotative, distant, hyper, just, mere, paranoid, reparative, slow, surface, symptomatic, uncritical, even large" (1).

As we shall see, the lexicon associated with close reading proved over time to be remarkably labile, by no means bound to the terminology or doctrinal adhesions of the New Criticism. The significance of this fluidity will concern me later. In the meantime, we can remark the contradictory aspect of close reading in retrospect: in the 1980s it was repudiated by scholars as a formalism sealing the literary work off from history or social context. Today new formalisms have emerged that enthusiastically embrace close reading, a development worth noting for its historical irony.[24]

Close reading, then, is a puzzling anachronism, a contradiction, even a scandal. When Derek Attridge and Henry Staten, for example, in their exemplary study *The Craft of Poetry*, set out to construct a model of "minimal interpretation," they declined to call this a version of close reading because this term had become "ideologically radioactive, and means too many different things."[25] Even if some scholars feel that it is time to rid the discipline of this discipline of this practice in favor of its apparent antagonist, "distant reading," that task has proven to be difficult, not only because close

24. See Caroline Levine, *Forms: Whole, Rhythm, Hierarchy, Network* (Princeton, NJ: Princeton University Press, 2017). Levine's work sums up a tendency of the previous two decades, provoking a wide-ranging reconsideration of form in literary theory, now purged of the ahistorical and apolitical character imputed to its earlier versions. More recently, Levine has suggested that while "close reading and historicism have been well-suited to interrupting habits and assumptions" in the twentieth century, the climate crisis requires "other methods," entailing "an expansive version of formalism, one that is drawn in part from the study of the arts but also reaches beyond the aesthetic." *The Activist Humanist: Form and Method in the Climate Crisis* (Princeton, NJ: Princeton University Press, 2023), 23.

25. Derek Attridge and Henry Staten, *The Craft of Poetry: Dialogues on Minimal Interpretation* (London: Routledge, 2015), 2.

reading is so entrenched in pedagogy, but also because it has become too diffuse to isolate for the purpose of excision.[26] In any case, we are forced to consider the possibility that something more is at stake in the return of close reading than yet another effort to rationalize disciplinary practice. Debate about close reading is driven today—as it was during the period of its origin—by concern with *reading itself* in the era of mass literacy. Reading in the modern era has never been static or internally homogeneous; it has evolved in response to a series of shocks to the system of communication, within which both reading and writing have been continually resituated. To this point I shall return.

The practice of close reading raises a further preliminary question about the relation between *reading*, as an ability possessed by the majority of the population, and *interpretation*, the most common name for disciplinary practice in literary study. Reading is a vastly larger domain of practice than interpretation and for the most part escapes government by the standards of academic literary study. Reading does not necessarily result in interpretation, much less in essays or monographs on works of literature. And yet, close reading gestures toward "reading" as a name for the practice that inaugurates the discipline of literary study as an interpretive practice in the interwar years of the twentieth century. The use of "reading" as another name for interpretation has the character of a trope, a metonymy. This troping of

26. The relation between close reading and distant reading constitutes an antagonism in the discipline, but in my view this antagonism is unnecessary. I argue at the end of this essay that distant reading was *called forth* by close reading (and vice versa) in a dialectical moment of the discipline's history.

interpretation as "reading" gives us our first clue to the history of close reading.[27]

In order better to appreciate the significance of "close reading" as a way of naming a core practice of literary study, it will help to recall the typical idiom of criticism in the centuries before I. A. Richards. In the long tradition of critical writing extending from Dryden to Eliot, there is very little close textual analysis to which one might point. This kind of analysis was to be found rather in the sphere of textual editing, which in turn assimilated a much older tradition of glossing or commentary.[28] Criticism was devoted, as I have

27. See P. M. Wetherill, *The Literary Text: An Examination of Critical Methods* (Berkeley: University of California Press, 1974), writing just when New Criticism was losing its hegemony in the discipline and just before the triumph of theory: "The job of the critic is in consequence more and more to *read*. Indeed, Cleanth Brooks calls his criticism *readings*" (xii).

28. The genre of commentary names a vast production from antiquity to the present, much of it devoted to the scripture of the monotheistic religions, often overlapping in the premodern world with the interpretation of law. Commentary on literary and philosophical works in antiquity and the medieval era was slightly less plentiful, though important culturally. For an excellent introduction to the commentary tradition, see *The Rhetoric of Cicero in its Medieval and Early Renaissance Commentary Tradition*, ed. Virginia Cox and John O. Ward (Leiden: Brill, 2006). Commentary was usually organized as the sequential explication of textual segments, a linear format that looks very unlike Anglo-American literary criticism of the twentieth century and later. Michel Foucault has some valuable remarks on commentary in his "Discourse on Language," in *The Archaeology of Knowledge*, trans. A. M. Sheridan Smith (New York: Pantheon, 1972): "The infinite rippling of commentary is agitated from within by the dream of masked repetition." Commentary, he continues, aspires "to say something other than the text itself, but on condition that it is the text itself which is uttered and, in some ways, finalized." In this way, commentary doubles back onto its origin in "recitation" (221). Despite the primal oral scene invoked by Foucault, we can define commentary in its various historical forms simply as *writing about writing*. In this sense, a work such as

remarked, chiefly to the aim of judgment. To bring this point out more clearly, I glance briefly here at a very small sample of predisciplinary critical discourse, which I take (somewhat arbitrarily) from an essay by Arthur Symons, "The Decadent Movement in Literature," published in 1893. Although the essay is more than usually substantive for the belletristic criticism of its time, I offer it as a typical example of criticism as a predisciplinary genre of writing. Here is a passage from the essay, in which Symons describes the poetry of Mallarmé:

> His early poems, "L'Après-midi d'un faune," "Hérodiade," for example, and some exquisite sonnets, and one or two fragments of perfectly polished verse, are written in a language which has nothing in common with every-day language—symbol within symbol, image within image; but symbol and image achieve themselves in expression without seeming to call for the necessity of a key. The latest poems (in which punctuation is sometimes entirely suppressed, for our further bewilderment) consist merely of a sequence of symbols, in which every word must be taken in a sense with which its ordinary significance has nothing to do. Mallarmé's contortion of the French language, so far as mere style is concerned, is curiously similar to the kind of depravation which was undergone by the Latin language in its decadence.[29]

Roland Barthes's *S/Z* can be seen as an extended riff on the commentary tradition. By contrast, as we shall see, close reading implies something different from writing about writing: a particular relation between writing and *reading*.

29. Arthur Symons, "The Decadent Movement in Literature," in *The Symbolist Movement in Literature*, ed. Matthew Creasy (Manchester: Carcanet Press, 2014), 169–183. I have excerpted these sentences from a longer paragraph on Mallarmé, also devoid of quotation. Symons's essay begins by citing

I ask the reader to set aside what Symons is asserting about Mallarmé and attend only to the typical features of this specimen of critical discourse. The sample offered here is by necessity extremely small, but it would not be wrong, I believe, to regard it as representative of most critical discourse at the turn of the twentieth century. Symons has without doubt read Mallarmé's poetry closely and carefully, and what he has to say ought not to be dismissed as mere "impressionism." And yet, the passage, like the essay as a whole, is notable for what is absent from it: any quotation from the poems, any reference to particular words, phrases, or lines that would support Symons's assertions about Mallarmé's style, or the larger significance of his language. The absence of these features obtains throughout Symons's discussion of Mallarmé, as also of the other authors whom he addresses in his essay. It does not occur to Symons that his argument needs quotation, much less that it requires an account of his procedure in reading Mallarmé. His reading occurs *in the background* of his writing and remains there, as with much criticism of the later nineteenth century.[30] Symons's criticism does not look

a few phrases from the poets he discusses, but the remainder of his essay is entirely without quotation. Quotation was not absent from criticism, especially the earlier nineteenth century, when the great reviews often included lengthy block quotations from novels, poetry, and other kinds of writing. On the use of long extracts, see Nicholas Dames, "On Not Close Reading: The Prolonged Excerpt as Critical Protocol," in *The Feeling of Reading: Affective Experience and Victorian Literature*, ed. Rachel Ablow (Ann Arbor: Michigan University Press, 2010), 11–26. Dames argues that in reviewing novels, these lengthy quotations were intended to produce the experience of reading the work, an experience characterized mainly in emotive terms. These quotations were not the occasion for close reading in the sense we mean today.

30. Chris Baldick, *Criticism and Literary Theory 1890 to the Present* (London: Longman, 1996), notes the visible difference of published criticism

disciplinary to us, just because of what is absent from it—not a careful reading of Mallarmé, which we can presume Symons has undertaken, but the *evidence* of this reading. This is a second clue to the origins of close reading as a disciplinary practice. Our understanding of this mode of reading, however, cannot advance further without stepping back at this point from the history of criticism to consider the question of reading in general.

TOWARD A GENERAL THEORY OF READING

Is this level of conceptual generality necessary in order to understand close reading? I believe that it is, despite the manifest scope of such a general theory. Close reading is (tautologically) a kind of reading, a particular kind of reading among many possible kinds of reading. Although it would be helpful to have at hand an exhaustive typology of reading practices for comparative purposes, I do not think we

---

by the end of the 1920s; by then, the pages of criticism had begun to be distinguished by frequent indented or in-sentence quotations (78). Jonathan Kramnick, in "Criticism and Truth," *Critical Inquiry* 47.2 (Winter 2021): 218–240, sees in-sentence quotation as the fundamental practice of criticism. The book-length version of this argument, *Criticism and Truth: On Method in Literary Studies* (Chicago: University of Chicago Press, 2023), elaborates this hypothesis into a powerful argument for the normative value of close reading as a "craft" practice, described figuratively as the "weaving" together of an alien literary text with the critic's own prose. Kramnick's "craft" is more or less identical to what I call in the argument to follow a *techne* or "art" in the generalized sense.

need that in order to proceed. What we need, rather, is a conceptualization of what reading is fundamentally, as a human practice. Building upon that definitional basis, we can go on to describe, as on a grid, the vertical hierarchy and horizontal dispersion of particular reading practices. That is, we will be able to account both for the status of any given reading practice in relation to a society's value terms and for the diffusion of any particular practice in a complex social environment in which different reading practices have different sites and do not necessarily interact with one another.

Close reading can be described, before any other particular features need be identified, as a *rare* practice, for the most part confined to the academy. It belongs at the upper end of the vertical hierarchy of sophisticated reading practices. It resides at the pole of dispersion defined by a small number of practitioners. By contrast, skimming or browsing practices of reading—characteristic of our engagement with newspapers, magazines, and many internet sites—are located at the pole of maximum dispersion. Somewhere in the middle we can locate the extracurricular reading of fiction, in which the reader is driven constantly forward, without pausing for closer inspection of the text. What we call "immersive reading" is *not* close reading, a point to which I shall return at the end of this essay. As a counterintuitive practice, close reading offers a specific kind of pleasure, more easily cultivated in the literature classroom than in the everyday reading of literate persons. Equipped with a general theory of reading, it will be possible for us to give an account of close reading's further institutional and ideological determinations, its social valences as a rarified practice, and its appearances and disappearances in literary study.

As a species of reading, close reading belongs ultimately to the genus of *methodized action*, an immense domain of human behavior. All forms of labor, for example, are methodized actions. Insofar as the human species has dedicated ever more of its time to labor, methodized actions have become ever greater in importance. This is one way of thinking about the necessity of schooling, which extends into adulthood and beyond. Reading requires instruction because it is inherently difficult—so difficult, in fact, that some people never acquire the ability to read, or at least never become comfortable integrating reading into their daily lives. At the same time, reading can be a form of relaxation after engagement in labor, a mildly laborious pleasure. The tension between these aspects of reading is a deep condition of close reading, which couples the reading of literature—a means of recreation—with a signifier connoting effort: "close," as in "close work." This conjunction provides another clue to the historical puzzle of close reading's origin as a disciplinary practice.

I will assume that any study of reading today must be grounded in the rapidly growing field of research in the neurophysiology and cognitive science of reading.[31] For these

31. Stanislas Dehaene, *Reading in the Brain: The Science and Evolution of a Human Invention* (New York: Viking, 2009), describes reading as a refunctioning of regions of the brain dedicated to recognizing visual signals of a particular sort, chiefly the edges or corners of objects; these form the basis for inscriptive marks. Although the neurons of the areas that accomplish reading were not evolved for the purpose of reading, the human brain learned reading and writing by developing a new way of correlating visual and aural information in the brain. Dehaene calls this "neuronal recycling" (144–148). The neuroscience of reading developed by Dehaene and his peers departs from earlier scientific research into reading, which was concerned with reading as observable bodily behavior, chiefly manifest as eye movements or "saccades." On the neuroscience of reading, see also Maryanne Wolf, *Proust and*

disciplines, reading is an action of the body, despite the fact that reading can look like inaction, the body at rest. The stillness of the reading body conceals intense activity in the brain. I offer here a description of reading that builds on the scientific basis for our understanding of reading as methodized action:

Reading is the coordinated action of human sensory, neurological, and motor systems for the purpose of using a technology of material inscription, or *writing*. All reading is the use of writing as an instrumentality and as such can be described with reference to how human beings use instruments or tools. Because the use of tools can be improved with practice, reading is, like all use of instruments, a skill, or, better, an *art*.

In one sense, I expect that this description will seem merely obvious, despite the otiose reference to neuroscience. And yet this is seldom where we scholars begin when we talk about reading. We begin, usually, with the notion of reading as an *interpretive* activity, that is, a rarified form of reading.[32]

---

the Squid: The Story and Science of Reading in the Brain (New York: Harper Perennial, 2007). For a study of reading from the perspective of cognitive science, see Daniel T. Willingham, *The Reading Mind: A Cognitive Approach to Understanding How the Mind Reads* (San Francisco: Jossey-Bass, 2017). For a sophisticated cognitive study of reading from the vantage of a literary critic, see Andrew Elfenbein, *The Gist of Reading* (Stanford, CA: Stanford University Press, 2018). Elfenbein looks at reading as the interplay between "automatic" and "controlled" responses, which permit readers to hold works in their minds as what he calls a "gist." Elfenbein is describing an ideal reading practice. Much reading, of course, does not survive in the memory for any length of time.

32. For a representative theory of reading as literary interpretation (one of many), see Wolfgang Iser, *The Act of Reading: A Theory of Aesthetic Response*

From this vantage, the notion that reading is an art is hardly controversial; but it is just the notion of art that drops out of our analysis of reading when we descend to the level at which reading is taught to children, where it is identified as *literacy*. There we are more likely to resort to the notion of reading as a skill, a concept that is inadequate for the purpose of a general theory of reading. On the one hand, "skill" fails to evoke the social prestige of art, while on the other, "art" fails to acknowledge the methodical or laborious nature of skilled practice. Reading must be understood, then, as both skill and art at all levels of practice—that is, from the conversion of alphabetic (or other) script into phonemes and thence into words all the way up to the most virtuoso hermeneutic performances, such as we find in Auerbach's *Mimesis* or Sedgwick's *Epistemology of the Closet*. Punctuating the trajectory of artistic development are moments of cognitive breakthrough, when reading ascends to a higher level of art. As scholars of literature, we usually name this higher level "interpretation," which implies something more complex than is indicated by the mere comprehension of sentences.

If reading is generally understood as a cognitive skill, this notion often permits us to ignore the fact that we read with our bodies.[33] The residually Cartesian dualism that still

---

(Baltimore, MD: Johns Hopkins University Press, 1978). For a study of non-disciplinary forms of reading, see *The Ethnography of Reading*, ed. Jonathan Boyarin (Berkeley: University of California Press, 1993). Elizabeth Long, in her contribution to that volume, "Textual Interpretation as Collective Action," notes that "academics tend to repress consideration of variety of reading practices due to our assumptions that everyone reads (or ought to) as we do professionally, privileging the cognitive, ideational, and analytic mode" (192).

33. See the important study by the Teagle Foundation, "What Is a Reader? A White Paper on Undergraduate Literacy and the Future of Literary Studies,"

pervades so much of our discourse about thought serves us very poorly in the context of reading. Everyone who teaches children how to read knows this, especially when there are impediments to reading such as dyslexia. At the level of interpretation, just as with basic reading, there are equally mysterious obstructions to reading. These typically arise, we like to say, from a failure to attend to the "words on the page," as though the reader were suffering in fact from an inability to see those words. The figure of "closeness" in the concept of close reading foregrounds, as we have already noted, a certain compensatory effort, a struggle to maintain consistency of attention as the eyes move across the page, collocating the jumps or saccades between each point of focus. This effort is not close reading, however—only the physiological basis for the familiar spatial trope.[34]

January 20, 2014, Tyrus Miller et al., https://www.teaglefoundation.org/ Teagle/media/GlobalMediaLibrary/documents/resources/What_is_a _Reader.pdf?ext=.pdf. These authors describe reading "as a practice involving cognitive functions, the body of the reader, and enabling technologies and social institutions" (12–13).

34. The spatial trope prevailed ultimately as the name for our normative disciplinary practice, but the temporal trope was favored by some, including Reuben Brower. See Brower, "The Humanities: Reading in Slow Motion," in *Reading for Life: Developing the College Student's Lifetime Reading Interest*, ed. Jacob M. Price (Ann Arbor: University of Michigan Press, 1959), 75–99; reprinted as "Reading in Slow Motion," in *In Defense of Reading: A Reader's Approach to Literary Criticism*, ed. Reuben Arthur Brower and Richard Poirier (New York: Dutton, 1962), 3–21. The temporal trope has a distinguished precedent in Nietzsche's well-known description of philology in *Daybreak* as slow reading. Like "close," the qualifier "slow" toggles between literal and figurative senses. Considered as an act, slow reading is difficult to specify. The pace of most reading is determined by a ratio between difficulty of comprehension and intensity of interest. With novels or other narrative forms, engaged or "immersive" reading tends to accelerate pace. Slow reading is often conflated with rereading,

The recognition of reading as an instance of embodied cognition is not likely at this date to encounter resistance, even if it is in practice often ignored. Much easier to acknowledge is the fact that reading takes as its object the product of another art: the art of writing. As a form of art, writing sprawls incoherently from amateur calligraphy to *Anna Karenina*. Nonetheless, there is a concept that encloses all of these versions of writing: production. Because writing and reading logically imply each other, reading too must be acknowledged as a productive art. Reading is the art of *making sense* of writing, an arduous transformative operation upon what are finally just marks on a surface.

Theorists of literacy describe reading as accomplished in two phases, which they call *decoding* and *comprehension*. By "decoding" is meant the conversion of marks on a surface, or graphemes, into phonemes and thence into words.[35] Phonemes are a long way from words; readers must make words out of phonemes. Decoding is fraught with obstacles that confront beginning readers with all sorts of puzzles, a consequence of the peculiar features of any writing

---

another action that has been proposed as equivalent to close reading. It would be easy to show, however, that rereading is undertaken in many circumstances unrelated to literary interpretation. Finally, I note that I do not engage here with the term "deep reading," which has some currency today, and which gestures nonspecifically toward all the modes of reading at the opposite pole from "shallow" practices such as skimming. As I have argued elsewhere—see John Guillory, "How Scholars Read," *ADE Bulletin* 146 (2008): 8–17—skimming is not always shallow, but can be employed as a scholarly practice.

35. The crucial function of phonemic recognition in learning to read is not universally acknowledged in the US educational system, which still widely favors the "whole language" method. This method has no support from current neuroscience and has probably impaired generations of readers. For a critique of whole-language pedagogy, see Dehaene, *Reading in the Brain*, 225–227.

system that render it at best an approximation of speech. By "comprehension" is meant the reader's achieved understanding of a written utterance, a cognitive state that is inherently difficult to verify.[36] Comprehension might be elicited by requesting a paraphrase, but it can remain silent.[37] Comprehension, as the task of making sense out of strings of words, is in turn a long way from what we call "interpretation"; as the product of disciplinary reading, the latter can be expressed in written form.[38] For most purposes, silent comprehension

36. Decoding is possible without comprehension. Milton notoriously taught his daughters to read to him in Latin by sounding out the words without comprehending their meanings. Neither decoding nor comprehension is simple, whatever the educational level. Reading aloud a passage from Book IV of *Gulliver's Travels*, a student of mine misread "sorrel nag" as "surreal nag." A mistake of decoding, yes; but what is more surreal than a talking horse? The effort of comprehension can sometimes distort decoding, as well as the reverse. Although close reading, as I will argue presently, takes as its point of departure the relation between comprehension and interpretation, structuralist linguistics sometimes attempted to ground interpretation in decoding itself, the level of the phonemic. For a noteworthy example, see Roman Jakobson and Claude Lévi-Strauss, "Baudelaire's 'Les Chats'" [1962], in Roman Jakobson, *Language in Literature*, ed. Krystyna Pomorska and Stephen Rudy (Cambridge, MA: Harvard University Press, 1987), 480–521.

37. Comprehension is coterminous with what Richards calls "construing" in the epigraph to this essay. As teachers, we acknowledge the distinction between comprehension and interpretation in many ways, perhaps most poignantly in response to that minor tragedy of literary pedagogy when a student erects an ingenious or even brilliant interpretation of a work on the foundation of an obvious misreading of a word or the syntax of a sentence. Often there is no question about the error. But misreading can be more complicated than a simple lexical or grammatical mistake; charges of misreading enter into disagreements between scholars all the time. See, for example, Marc Redfield, "Professing Literature: John Guillory's Misreading of Paul de Man," *Romantic Circles* (May 2005).

38. "Interpretation" is a concept with a much broader domain of application than its use in literary study. Wider still is the concept of "understanding,"

is sufficient for a reader to function in our society.[39] Yet, for many, reading either stalls at this level or fails altogether when the reader is confronted with writing of any complexity, such as a literary text. As we shall see, the difficulties impeding comprehension give us another clue to the origins of close reading.

TECHNE, TECHNIQUE, TECHNOLOGY

The ability to read is transmitted across generations as what I will call, following the anthropologist Marcel Mauss, a

---

which can be a synonym for interpretation in many contexts of language use at the same time that it can function as an equivalent for simple comprehension of a written or oral communication. The semantic overlap between these terms is difficult to control. I attempt here to distinguish consistently between comprehension and interpretation, while bracketing understanding as the more general concept in this conceptual cluster.

39. The problem of comprehension is a point of connection in my argument with the emergence of a "close reading" practice alongside the institution of the Common Core State Standards. The phrase "close reading" is invoked only once in the Standards themselves, but it seems to be implied in the Core documents' account of reading. This is why the institution of the Standards was quickly followed by many books and articles advocating for a mode of reading that resembles New Criticism. In general, this version of close reading seeks to move away from the dominant reading pedagogy in primary and secondary schools, which is focused on "reader response," that is, on treating the text as a prompt for making "connections" with the life of the student. The new emphasis on "close reading" attempts to direct readers back to the text by the use of questions with "text dependent" answers, an aim that aligns with the prescriptions of the Common Core. See the Newstok bibliography for further comment.

cultural technique, a set of methodical actions that accomplish specified ends, that alter something in our environment or in ourselves. Technique, which alludes etymologically to its origin in the Greek concept of *techne*, or art, gestures forward to technology and reminds us that technique often involves the use of material instruments.[40] The study of "cultural technique" developed by Mauss in the earlier twentieth century has since become an important field in the human sciences, though it has only recently been taken up by literary theorists. I invoke in this essay the general findings of the theory, beginning with Mauss's description of the domain of techniques: "What emerges very clearly from them [techniques] is the fact that we are everywhere faced with physio-psycho-sociological assemblages of series of actions. These actions are more or less habitual and more or less ancient in the life of the individual and the history of the society."[41] Mauss studies the ways in which human beings

40. The descent of the term "technology" from the concept of *techne* is a complicated story. In later antiquity, rhetoric and related arts of language came to be called collectively the *technai logon*, the arts of speech. These two words were conflated into one Latin word, *technologia*. It is not easy to trace how the word for the "arts of speech" evolved into our concept of technology, but the path to the vernacular term is well documented. See the account of Leo Marx, "'Technology': The Emergence of a Hazardous Concept," *Social Research* 64.3 (Fall 1997): 965–988.

41. From Marcel Mauss, "Techniques of the Body" (1934), in *Marcel Mauss: Techniques, Technology and Civilization*, ed. Nathan Schlanger (New York: Durkheim Press, 2006), 92. For a study of cultural techniques, see Bernhard Siegert, *Cultural Techniques: Grids, Filters, Doors, and other Articulations of the Real*, trans. Geoffrey Winthrop-Young (New York: Fordham University Press, 2015). Siegert's choice of techniques might seem unusual, but he wants to stress the nonliterary origin of technique. In early human society, technique was developed most consequentially in the domain of agriculture, the precursor to all modern domains of culture.

instrumentalize their bodies in order to perform certain actions methodically, such as swimming or running. The most consequential such instrumentalization occurs with speech, an extraordinarily complex refunctioning of brain and bodily capabilities. The first tool for humans is thus the body itself. Eventually the process of instrumentalization is externalized in the creation of tools out of inorganic matter, the use of which constitutes a world of arts. Reading is, like many arts, a hybrid instrumentalization, involving both the material form of inscription (a tool) and a refunctioning of the visual and auditory processing of the brain, turning the brain, as Stanislas Dehaene writes, into a "reading device" (150).

The concept of "technique" both transliterates and translates *techne*, understood to include all productive practices, all making—in the context of the word's Greek origin, everything from the making of drinking vessels and houses to the making of poems and plays. Once the concept of technique is

---

In agriculture, we find techniques such as "irrigation, drainage, enclosure, and river regulation" (209). Writing and reading are techniques that come later, and it is only very much later that these practices are linked to the concept of culture in the sense of higher intellectual or artistic activity. On the preconceptual history of these later cultural techniques, Siegert cites the media theorist Thomas Macho: "Cultural techniques—such as writing, reading, painting, counting, making music—are always older than the concepts that are generated from them" (11). See Thomas Macho, "Zeit und Zahl: Kalender-und Zeitrechnung als Kulturtechniken," in *Bild—Schrift—Zahl*, ed. Sybille Krämer and Horst Bredekamp (Munich: Wilhelm Fink Verlag, 2003), 179. In the deeper background of my argument is the trilogy of books by Bernard Stiegler, *Technics and Time*, especially vol. 1, *The Fault of Epimetheus*, trans. Richard Beardsworth and George Collins (Stanford, CA: Stanford University Press, 1998). Stiegler's substitution of "technics" for Heidegger's "being" establishes a basis for understanding reading as the use of a writing technology.

specified, it is easy to see that both reading and writing must fall within its province. This point is the core thesis of the major work of André Leroi-Gourhan, *Gesture and Speech*, published in 1964, from which I cite a summary statement: "This gradual triumph of tools is inseparable from that of language—indeed the two phenomena are but one, just as technics and society form but one subject. As soon as writing became exclusively a means of phonetic recording of speech, language was placed on the same level as technics."[42] Extrapolating the inexorable development of technics into the future, Leroi-Gourhan speculated that the human species was on the cusp of replacing writing with audiovisual media of communication.[43] This apocalypse of writing—and

42. André Leroi-Gourhan, *Gesture and Speech*, trans. Anna Bostock Berger (Cambridge, MA: MIT Press, 1993), 211.

43. Leroi-Gourhan, *Gesture and Speech*, 212–213. And: "The preservation of thought can now be envisaged otherwise than in books, which will not offer the advantages of quick and easy manageability for very much longer. Preselected and instantaneously reconstituted information will soon be delivered by a huge magnetic storage facility with electronic selection. For centuries yet, reading will go on being important—although significantly less so for the majority of human beings—but writing will be doomed to disappear rapidly, to be replaced by dictaphonic equipment with automatic printing. . . . Writing will enter the infrastructure without changing the functioning of the intellect, as a transitional stage that will have been dominant for a few thousand years" (403). *Gesture and Speech* was a major influence on Derrida, who read the book shortly before composing *Of Grammatology*. Reading Leroi-Gourhan with Derrida, we might hypothesize that writing, like other media, is best understood from the vantage of its technological obsolescence. The end of writing does not mean that writing will actually disappear, any more than candles disappeared after gas and electric lighting arrived. The end story of writing might even be told conversely as the spread of writing to all areas of human life, where it functions so differently than in its past as to constitute an "end" of its earlier form. For a version of this converse story, see Deborah Brandt's sociological study, *The Rise of Writing: Defining Mass Literacy* (Cambridge:

therefore of reading—has not yet occurred, nor does it seem likely. But this is not to say that writing and reading in the modern world have not been subject to massive shocks. As the ability to read and write has been nearly universalized, so has it been trivialized in many of its sites, a development accelerated by our constantly advancing technologies of communication. These instrumentalities, for example, have vacated the premise for the familiar letter, a form in which writing of enduring interest was produced for millennia. The fate of the private letter was sealed with the invention of the telephone, although it survived some decades beyond this invention. In the place of the letter today, we have the ephemeral forms of email and text message. Adjusting techniques of reading to kinds of writing is no longer so easy as it was when all writing was rare and very little of it was preserved. It is an illusion of the history of writing that it seems to consist of so much literature and philosophy and other genres

---

Cambridge University Press, 2015). Brandt argues for the emergence of a new relation between writing and reading, which she calls "writing over reading," a relation expressed by interviewees in her research as "a simple preference for writing compared to reading, liking to write more than liking to read" (95–96). For a major philosophical statement on the end of writing, see Vilém Flusser, *Does Writing Have a Future?*, trans. Nancy Ann Roth (Minneapolis: University of Minnesota Press, 2011). Flusser answers the question of his title with a hard "no": "Writing, in the sense of placing letters and other marks one after another, appears to have little or no future" (3). Flusser contends that writing is being replaced by "technical images" encoded in "tapes, records, films, videotapes, or computer disks" (1)—already today an outdated list of new technologies. He concludes in a later chapter, "What we fear, as we anticipate the most perfect form and the end of alphabetic writing, is the decline of reading, that is, of critical decoding" (77). Flusser's argument is not as simple as his apocalyptic rhetoric implies, but I cannot here take up the question as he frames it. I offer a further comment at the end of this essay on the mutual implication of reading and writing.

of permanent interest. A question about the superfluity of ephemeral writing lurks beneath the fate of reading in literary study—another clue to the origins of close reading. This question is forced upon us by the technological condition in which the reading of literature in the modern world occurs. Despite the massive proliferation of writing, even of writing that belongs to literary genres, only an extremely tiny fraction of it will attract sufficient interest to provoke an effort to read closely.[44]

The real-world diversity of relations between reading and writing determines what I will call the specific *technicity* of these relations, the particular interaction of *techne*, technique, and technology in any practice of writing, or correlated practice of reading. I turn first to the concept of *techne* in order to elucidate this complexity further. Scholars usually invoke this term with reference to Aristotle's famous account in the *Nicomachean Ethics*, offered in the course of his discussion of the different types of knowledge. As the knowledge of how to do or make something, *techne* is distinguished from *episteme*, scientific knowledge. *Episteme* is knowledge of the world that can be demonstrated with

44. Although literary writing is only a small fraction of all writing, it is accumulating rapidly in absolute volume. In this context the most striking development is the vast new industry of internet self-publication. Nearly all of this literary writing will be read by no more than a handful of readers, or no readers at all. Does writing in this form already exceed the "great unread" of literary writing descending to us from the age of print? If so, this suggests a new function for literary writing, which is not to be read, but something else; whatever this function is, it seems to expire in the moment of writing's production. For a revelatory study of the new world of self-publication, see Mark McGurl, *Everything and Less: The Novel in the Age of Amazon* (New York: Verso, 2021).

certainty. Crucially, *techne* and *episteme* are both forms of knowledge. Aristotle also recognizes *techne* as an instance of learned or nonintuitive practice, a form of *reason*—that is, *techne* requires thought about how an action is to be performed in order to achieve an end: "Now since building is an art [*techne*] and is essentially a reasoned state of capacity to make, and there is neither any art that is not such a state nor any such state that is not an art, *art* [*techne*] is identical with a state of capacity to make, involving a true course of reasoning" (*Nicomachean Ethics*, 1140a).[45] "Reasoned state" means here what we would call a mode of cognition, a particular form of "practical reason." Importantly, this mode of cognition might or might not involve abstract concepts, a fact that has proven to be a source of confusion about its status as a mode of reason. As we shall see, this aspect of *techne* has important consequences for the history of close reading, which, as we know, has mysteriously resisted conceptual definition.

Techne as a mode of practical reason—with or without concepts—is directed toward the improvement of technique, or *efficiency*, to use a term often employed by Mauss. A simple example of what efficiency means can be seen in the different ways in which the hands and eyes are engaged with the

45. Aristotle, *Nicomachean Ethics*, in *The Complete Works of Aristotle*, 2 vols., ed. Jonathan Barnes (Princeton, NJ: Princeton University Press, 1985), 2:1799–1800. My invocation of Aristotle is not intended to reinstate old theory. In fact, the concept of *techne* points the way forward to a general revision of aesthetics, perhaps finally post-Romantic. See Henry Staten, *Techne Theory: A New Language for Art* (London: Bloomsbury Academic, 2019). For a study of "technicity" as an immemorial aspect of human life, see Arthur Bradley, *Originary Technicity: The Theory of Technology from Marx to Derrida* (London: Palgrave Macmillan, 2011).

technology of the typewriter or electronic keyboard. "Touch-typing" is a technique that permits the use of all ten fingers and does not require one to look at the keyboard. Is "hunt and peck" also a technique? It seems by comparison more intuitive, slower, and hence less efficient. The point here is that the line between intuitive practice and technique is difficult to determine. The transition from unmethodical action to technique shifts back and forth across a wavering threshold. In the case of reading, improving its efficiency as technique can make basic literacy seem merely intuitive. Yet there is no such thing as a wholly intuitive mode of reading. All reading is methodical action; the more complex the method, the greater the energy cost to the body.[46]

Reading and writing as cultural techniques are difficult to master, even at the simplest level of practice. For this reason, the project of universalizing literacy in the modern world required an enormous social investment. But "literacy" is far from an adequate concept for our relation to the diverse objects of reading and writing, including street signs, graffiti, texting, instructions, newspapers, magazine articles, editorials, blogs, online posts, letters, emails, novels, poems, plays, essays, histories, legal briefs, memos, bureaucratic forms, statistical reports, philosophical arguments, scholarly treatises, scientific papers. It is absurd to suppose that literacy guarantees even the comprehension of all these forms of writing.

These examples also remind us that complexity is not just a feature of literary discourse, nor is it exactly the same as

46. See Leroi-Gourhan, *Gesture and Speech*, 404, for a discussion of reading as "mentally exhausting."

difficulty. The difficulty of reading and writing in some contexts inheres precisely in its effort to *reduce* the complexity of speech, to arrest its hypercontextualized flow in ways that prevent disasters of miscommunication. This kind of "informational" writing has its proper art and is not necessarily easy to master; nor is it always easy to read. We need only reflect on the occasions in which a piece of informational prose, a memo or an email, becomes contested, inaugurating an urgent effort of parsing. This effort has little to do with what we think of as literary interpretation. Literary genres of writing, by contrast, are crowded at a pole of writing possessed of inherent complexity, even when the language appears to be simple; these modes of writing sometimes risk unintelligibility, which is to say that comprehension is never simply assured with the act of decoding.

CLOSE READING
AS TECHNIQUE

The puzzles generated by our efforts to define close reading are the result of our failure to understand its operation as technique. A better understanding of technique will enable us to distinguish precisely between close reading and other techniques of reading closely, of which there have been many historically and in our own time. These other techniques might address other kinds of texts than the literary, such as religious or legal works; or they might define other ways of reading literature, such as *explication de texte* or the mode of criticism illustrated above in my quotation from Arthur

Symons.[47] The disciplinary practice of close reading is only one mode of reading closely.

Historians of literary study have been frustrated by the difficulty of defining the actual procedure of close reading, usually defaulting to the notion of reading with "attention to the words on the page." This very general notion, however, is too broad to account for the specificity of close reading as technique, or its history in departments of literature in the twentieth century and after. The problem of defining close reading is the corollary of the question with which I began this essay: why was

---

47. The difference between close reading and *explication de texte* is worth clarifying here, as it has been the occasion of perennial confusion. The French technique is a late efflorescence of the commentary tradition, its ultimate formalization. Close reading, as we shall see, is a break with this tradition, and a break with its disciplinary avatar, literary history. As a school exercise, *explication de texte* can take the form of questions that have answers grounded in literary history or philology. A description of how to carry out this procedure can be found in Gustave Lanson's classic 1910 essay, "La méthode de l'histoire littéraire," which reduces the technique to a list of questions, beginning with whether a text is authentic, whether it is complete, its date, and the history of its editions, before proceeding on to other philological and historical questions: "On établira ensuite le sens littéral du texte. Le sens des mots et des tours par l'histoire de la langue, la grammaire et la syntaxe historique. Les sens des phrases, par l'éclaircissement des rapports obscurs, des allusions historiques ou biographiques." Having established answers to these questions, the student might address more critical matters: "Quel a été le succès, quelle a été l'influence de l'oeuvre?" In *Essais de méthode, de critique et d'histoire littéraire*, ed. Henri Peyre (Paris: Hachette, 1965), 43–45. For a critique of the method, see Roland Barthes's essay of 1969, "Reflections on a Manual," in *The Rustle of Language*, trans. Richard Howard (Berkeley: University of California Press, 1989), 22–28. For an argument recommending *explication de texte* in Anglo-American literary study implicitly as an alternative to the New Criticism, see Leo Spitzer, *A Method of Interpreting Literature* (Northampton, MA: Smith College, 1949).

close reading not generally acknowledged by this name until sometime after the fact of its dissemination? I offer a hypothesis here in partial response to this question: the belatedness of the term of art confirms the fact that literary critics were struggling to understand their reading practice *as technique*, as a practice that crossed a threshold from the (more) intuitive to the (more) technical. By understanding close reading as a practice both rarified and technical, it will be possible to specify its determinations in the history of the Anglo-American university. This institutional history is punctuated by the moments of close reading's emergence, dissemination, apparent eclipse, and return—the last phase signaling a crisis of sorts, when disciplinary reading itself is called into question.

Foregrounding the problem of technique confirms and deepens the insight of Alan Brown in his important essay of 1999, "On the Subject of Practical Criticism," which identifies the central contradiction of practical criticism (Brown uses this term interchangeably with "close reading"): "The history of practical criticism as an examinatory structure can indeed be read as a series of variations on the unresolved tension between competing, or mutually exclusive elements: between technique and personal response, between objective knowledge and subjective integrity, 'analysis' and 'judgment.'"[48] Brown looks at the long-term effect of practical criticism on A-level exams.[49] These exams demand technique

48. Alan Brown, "On the Subject of Practical Criticism," *The Cambridge Quarterly* 28.4 (January 1999): 301.

49. Did Richards's course also improve the performance of his students on the tripos? We know that the lectures behind *Practical Criticism* were hugely popular, and that the students often spilled out into the street. It is not implausible that students made a connection between the course and their performance on the tripos.

and a methodical approach to reading; at the same time, students are expected to go beyond technique to express a cultivated sensibility opposed to "the 'technologico-Benthamite' edifice of Ricardian theory" (308).[50] Brown invokes Leavis's resistance to Richards's emphasis on technique: "the idea of technique, as such, comes under suspicion" (308). As Leavis writes in his response to Ezra Pound's *How to Read*, "Everything must start from the training of sensibility, together with the equipping of the student against the snares of 'technique.'"[51] Brown notes that students were expected to resolve

50. Richards speaks in *Practical Criticism* of the "communicative efficiency" (51) of good poems, just the sort of locution that for his critics betrayed his utilitarianism.

51. F. R. Leavis, *How to Teach Reading: A Primer for Ezra Pound* (Cambridge: Minority Press, 1932), 25. Leavis's notion of the "training of sensibility" brings the latter term into a complicated but necessary relation to "judgment." Sensibility in the discourse of the interwar critics manifestly serves as the ground of judgment, but it is not on the same level of abstraction. In Richards's terms, sensibility is an organization of impulses and attitudes, specifically a neurological state. But it also circulates for him and others as a name for certain historical conditions, as in Eliot's "dissociation of sensibility." Judgment is the operation—the act—that expresses sensibility. For complex reasons, the English critics were more likely to emphasize the sensibility-judgment complex than their American peers, a point I address further below. The invocation of "Bentham" that hovers over this moment in British criticism is a hint about the historical precursors of sensibility. Even for Eliot, this moment betrays a certain assimilation of the Romantics in their opposition to utilitarianism and to the perceived depravations of industrial civilization. Joseph North, in *Literary Criticism: A Concise Political History* (Cambridge, MA: Harvard University Press, 2017), offers to revive the cultivation of sensibility, the origin of which he imputes largely to I. A. Richards, as a solution to current impasses in literary study. For a different sense of this history, positing a Romantic lineage for sensibility by way of a memorial assimilation of Wordsworth in I. A. Richards's work, see James Chandler, "The Question of Sensibility," *New Literary History* 49.4 (Autumn 2018): 467–492.

this conflict by finding the "precise balance between personal response and technique," an expectation that resulted in a classic double bind (308). The demand for technique was answered by the production of manuals offering students models for practical criticism, guides that continued to be produced long thereafter.[52] No guide, however, could ensure the rightness of a student's "personal response."

Brown's is a persuasive analysis, which I would amend only by suggesting that the technique of reading he describes need not be reduced to a mimesis of "technologico-Benthamite" production. That ideological content is superimposed on a technicity that is an immemorial aspect of human life, and belies the reduction of technique to an imitation of industrial production only.[53] As we will see, both

52. See Brown's discussion of a study guide produced in 1995 by John Peck and Martin Coyle, *How to Study: Practical Criticism* (Brown, "On the Subject of Practical Criticism," 300–307). For an overview addressed to preparation for A-levels, see Margaret Mathieson, *Teaching Practical Criticism: An Introduction* (London: Croom Helm, 1985).

53. The connection between close reading as technique and industrial production is not wrong, even if technique is an immemorial fact of human life. Richards notoriously opened his *Principles of Literary Criticism* with the assertion that "a book is a machine to think with," echoing Le Corbusier, and invoking the technoindustrial milieu whose effects he was also trying to remediate. The confusion about how the technique of reading was related to its technological environment was similarly pervasive as the New Criticism was disseminated. For example, a report composed for the Commission on Secondary School Curriculum, *Language in Education* (New York: D. Appleton-Century, 1940), connected close textual interpretation with speed reading, associating the technique too simply with its technological environment: "It seems to us questionable practice to train for speed in reading without at the same time giving attention to the techniques of interpretation. Although there are no experimental data available, we should expect the speed of reading to increase with practice in close interpretation" (208). This confusion persists in the much later Teagle white paper, "What Is a Reader?," in which

writing and reading come to be perceived in the modern world as industrialized, provoking complicated and sometimes contradictory responses in the literary professoriate. On the main point, nonetheless, Brown is right: the central problem of literary study in the twentieth century was the problem of technique—the technique of *reading*. And he is further right that practical criticism was conflicted about technique, desiring at once to produce it, and yet to transcend it.[54]

In the United States, the problem of technique played out somewhat differently. Here there was no precise equivalent to A-levels or the Cambridge tripos, and technique had another role: to establish the professional status of the cadre of literary critics in the university, distinguishable as a group from the literary historians who dominated the modern

---

the authors criticize close reading as an imitation of the industrial mode of production. They endorse an argument by Alex Reid in a blog post entitled "Robot Graders, New Aesthetic, and the End of the Close Reading Industry": "I think the 'close reading' model that dominates English . . . is ultimately linked with computer grading and industrial modes of attention"; https://profalexreid.com/2012/04/18/robot-graders-new-aesthetic-and-the-end-of-the-close-reading-industry/. For a discussion of speed reading, see Adrian Johns, *The Science of Reading: Information, Media, and Mind in Modern America* (Chicago: University of Chicago Press, 2023), 258–269.

54. Alexander Pope's famous phrase, "a grace beyond the reach of art," from *An Essay on Criticism* (1711), part 1, 155, suggests that the contradiction Brown observes is inherent in all technique. Brown notes that students sometimes resorted in their practical criticism papers to rehearsing a lot of background information, in the hope of impressing their examiners. In fact, this strategy could lead examiners to downgrade a paper (310). For a clarifying discussion of the philosophical background to this problem, see Marieke M. A. Hendricksen, "'Art and Technique Always Balance the Scale': German Philosophies of Sensory Perception, Taste, and Art Criticism, and the Rise of the Term *Technik*, ca. 1735–ca. 1835," *History of Humanities* 2.1 (Spring 2017): 201–219.

language departments during this period. The American New Critics appropriated Richards's emphasis on technique, but not Leavis's revision in favor of an ineffable sensibility that transcended mere technique. On the contrary, the New Critics strongly emphasized the technique of reading as the basis for asserting criticism as a *specialized knowledge*, what I have described elsewhere as a claim to disciplinary jurisdiction over the verbal work of art.[55] As always, Cleanth Brooks makes the most explicit case on behalf of the critic in opposition to the literary historian, whom he describes in a passage from his essay "Literary History vs. Criticism" in *The Kenyon Review*:

> He [the English professor] has been trained (if he comes from one of our better universities) in linguistics and the history of literature. He possesses a great deal of information, valuable and interesting in its own right, and of incalculable value for the critic. But he himself is not that critic. He has little or no knowledge of the inner structure of a poem or a drama (this is not to say that he does not know the past critical generalizations on it!); he is ignorant of its architecture; in short, he often does not know how to *read*.[56]

55. See Guillory, *Professing Criticism*, 54. The historical problem here is the different time line for the professionalization of criticism in the United Kingdom and the United States. For American universities, professionalization proceeded more rapidly and superseded the model of the internally exiled critic, the figure represented in Leavis's vexed relation to Cambridge University.

56. Cleanth Brooks, "Literary History vs. Criticism," *The Kenyon Review* 2.4 (Autumn 1940): 405.

What does it mean to say that the professors do not know how to read? This is hyperbole, of course; yet it is not easy to unpack the trope. What Brooks really means is that the professors lack a technique of reading adequate to the work of literature. This technique of reading had no generally acknowledged name; nonetheless, the literary historians were able to recognize it as different from their own practice.[57]

For some reason, the New Critics consistently failed (or declined) to specify programmatically the technique of reading they believed they had extrapolated from hints in Richards's practice, or even to name it. Although this technique dispensed with Richards's psychologism, it appeared to early observers as an imitation of scientific method, a misrecognition, we are now able to say, of technicity as such.[58] Not a simulacrum of scientific practice, the New Critics rather offered *exemplary readings*, performances of reading such as

57. Were the literary historians so indifferent to the technique of reading as Brooks implies? It seems likely that their classroom practice diverged less from that of the New Critics than is evident in their published scholarship, which necessarily emphasized the results of their historical research. For an inquiry into the divergence between classroom practice and scholarship, see Rachel Sagner Buurma and Laura Heffernan, *The Teaching Archive: A New History for Literary Studies* (Chicago: University of Chicago Press, 2021). The New Critics were perhaps unusual in exploiting the possibilities of classroom procedure in their theory. Their formalization of these procedures is acknowledged in Hugh Kenner's dismissive essay, "The Pedagogue as Critic," in *The New Criticism and After*, ed. Thomas Daniel Young (Charlottesville: University Press of Virginia, 1976): "the curious thing is how a classroom strategy could come to mistake itself for a critical discipline" (45).

58. John Holloway's remark (see n. 12 above) is typical of the perception of New Criticism as wittingly or unwittingly scientistic. For an argument asserting the long-term influence of social science on New Criticism, see Joshua Gang, "Behaviorism and the Beginnings of Close Reading," *ELH* 78.1 (Spring 2011): 1–25.

we find in Brooks's *The Well Wrought Urn*, or Brooks and Warren's *Understanding Poetry*, in the latter taking the form of a series of leading questions. They nowhere established a precise formula for reading, but everywhere assumed that their mode of reading was imitable.[59]

Importantly, the technique of reading that helped the New Critics assert their expertise stopped short of application to judgment as such, leaving open the status of judgment as a province of individual sensibility. Judgment of literary works was validated indirectly, however, by the capacity of the critics' technique of reading to disclose the aesthetic essence of these works, their distinction as artistic creations from the products of industrial civilization. Although the orientation of criticism toward the ultimate aim of judgment persisted for a long time in the United Kingdom, it faded from the practice of American criticism by the mid-century, leaving behind only the technique of reading. This is why,

59. George Whalley, "Scholarship and Criticism," in *Academic Discourse*, ed. John J. Enck (New York: Appleton-Century-Crofts, 1964), looks back on this moment: "The New Criticism can be seen as one of the first successful attempts (based on Richards) to establish a pedagogic technique that would work in a practical way—in the lecture room" (156). Whalley's essay first appeared as "Scholarship and Criticism," *University of Toronto Quarterly* 29.1 (October 1959): 33–45. Steven Schryer, in *Fantasies of the New Class: Ideologies of Professionalism in Post–World War II American Fiction* (New York: Columbia University Press, 2011), rightly links close reading to the problem of technique: "Close reading became the discipline's specialized techne, its claim to professional identity, and the New Critics linked this techne to the imagined moral effects of literature in modern society" (31). This point is developed by Andrew Kopec, "The Digital Humanities, Inc.: Literary Criticism and the Fate of a Profession," *PMLA* 131.2 (March 2016): 324–339. Kopec opposes New Criticism's *techne* to digital criticism's mode of processing text, a point to which I will return at the end of this argument.

when we look back on this period, close reading appears to loom so large; it was a precipitation of multiple conflicts, both ideological and institutional—conflicts that receded from view with their apparent resolution in a normative disciplinary practice.

Although the term "close reading" in itself can suggest little more than careful attention to the words on the page, its emergence had other determinations we can begin to examine. Most obviously, close reading in the American university was inextricably linked to the category of literature as the primary object of the modern language disciplines. The complexity of the struggle to define this object can be measured by one of its early curricular casualties: the essay. Formerly unquestioned as a genre of literature, the essay came to be regarded by the New Critics as a propositional form of writing, not easily assimilated to the aesthetic ontology of the literary work.[60] Literature was constructed by this ontology for the purpose of its study in the university, an operation that had further institutional consequences—among them the relegation of critical writing itself to the category of the propositional, disqualifying it as a form of literary expression.

60. Tara Lockhart, "Teaching with Style: Brooks and Warren's Literary Pedagogy," in *Rereading the New Criticism*, ed. Miranda B. Hickman and John D. McIntyre (Columbus: Ohio State University Press, 2012), 195–217, examines Brooks and Warren's repeated attempt to grapple with the contradictory aesthetic status of the essay in successive editions of their anthology, *An Approach to Literature*, from 1936 to 1964. This struggle paralleled a real decline in the literary fortunes of the essay, which has only recently made a comeback in the form (along with memoir) of "creative nonfiction." The infelicity of this concept is the legacy of unresolved problems in New Criticism's effort to define literature.

The relation between literature and criticism was in this way mutually constitutive in the interwar period.

Despite the institutional advantages for the critics of these redefinitions, criticism suffered in consequence an internal division from which it never recovered, a parting of the ways between criticism as a technique of reading and criticism as an act of judgment. The downstream effect of this divergence was to bracket judgment itself, after the period of its initial deployment in the various "revaluations" proposed in both British and American venues of interwar criticism.[61] The works revalued upward, such as the metaphysical poets, or downward, such as the Romantics, were judged in part according to their *perceived responsiveness to a technique of reading*. But this was only a transitional phase of the discipline, a temporary correlation of judgment and technique. As the social investments of the New Criticism lost their force in later years, judgment itself came to be a secondary concern of criticism, tacitly assumed for a stabilized curriculum of literary works.[62] If the critics never wholly relinquished their claim to judgment, they no longer needed to engage in judgments about literary works in

61. For the principal statements, see F. R. Leavis, *New Bearings in English Poetry* (London: Chatto & Windus, 1932); F. R. Leavis, *Revaluation: Tradition & Development in English Poetry* (New York: George W. Stewart, 1947); Cleanth Brooks, *Modern Poetry and the Tradition* (Charlotte: University of North Carolina Press, 1939).

62. The repudiation of judgment as the main purpose of criticism was common by the 1950s, but its most sophisticated statement can be found in Northrop Frye, "Polemical Introduction," in *Anatomy of Criticism: Four Essays* (Princeton, NJ: Princeton University Press, 1957). Frye was not an exponent of New Criticism, but his project, like the New Critics', was premised on the redefinition of criticism as an interpretive rather than evaluative enterprise.

order to assert their identity as experts. For that purpose, they could rely largely on a technique of reading.

SHOWING THE WORK
OF READING

Despite the prevalence in literary study of the technique called "close reading," there is, even today, no real consensus about its constituent features. Peter Middleton offers a typical characterization of close reading as "a heterogeneous and largely unorganized set of practices and assumptions."[63] The mode of reading that survived the decline of New Criticism was and is, in the terms of my analysis, a minimally formalized technique. Close reading never acquired the procedural formality of other scholarly practices, such as *explication de texte* or textual editing. This is the reason scholars of the postwar period looked back uneasily on what they took to be the formal basis of their practice, which seemed to be at once methodical and yet too loosely codified. For this reason, too, even as close reading facilitated the integration of sophisticated new theoretical schemas into scholarship, it was relegated as a discrete practice to the introductory level of literary study.

Whatever name we give it, a technique of reading permanently transformed literary study during the interwar period. We might identify this transformation with the movement

63. Peter Middleton, *Distant Reading: Performance, Readership, and Consumption in Contemporary Poetry* (Tuscaloosa: University of Alabama Press, 2005), 5.

called New Criticism, but I believe it can be understood in a deeper sense as a moment in which the reading of literature was problematized across the Anglo-American system. Without doubt this event was a response to the massification of literacy, ongoing since the nineteenth century. In his 1939 essay, "Some Motifs in Baudelaire," Walter Benjamin offers a pithy statement of this new condition: "The crowd—no subject was more entitled to the attention of nineteenth-century writers. It was getting ready to take shape as a public in broad strata who had acquired facility in reading."[64] The emergence in the twentieth century of cultural works in new media forms such as film, radio, and television generated further anxiety, exacerbating a tendency toward declinist narratives.[65] Literary critics were forced to confront the rarity of literature as one form of writing among many in the modern world, and writing as one medium among many. This engagement was equally urgent in modernist writing itself, which was everywhere marked by an ambivalent struggle with mass media, including the forms of mass or popular writing.[66]

64. Walter Benjamin, "Some Motifs in Baudelaire," in *Charles Baudelaire: A Lyric Poet in the Era of High Capitalism*, trans. Harry Zohn (London: Verso, 1973), 120.

65. The massification of literacy inevitably appeared to contemporary observers as a decline in reading skills and led to regular social panics. For an account of this phenomenon, see Johns, *The Science of Reading*, 191–200. Assertions of decline in the general level of culture were ubiquitous during this period. For the most serious study of its time, see Q. D. Leavis, *Fiction and the Reading Public* (London: Chatto & Windus, 1939).

66. The emergence by the end of the nineteenth century of popular forms such as the "penny dreadfuls" and "shilling shockers" was a condition for modernist reaction, as scholars have long recognized. The full emergence of "genre" forms of writing—detective fiction, romance—further complicated the circumstances for the recognition of "serious" literature. For a classic study of the split between high and low cultural forms, which gave rise to the modern

Glancing briefly one last time at I. A. Richards's work of the 1920s, let us recall that Richards's task was to persuade his peers that the reading of literature was a problem, that its success had been taken for granted: "we discover what a comparatively relaxed and inattentive activity our reading of established poetry is."[67] His experiment in *Practical Criticism* disclosed a failure in the transmission of reading as technique: "A better technique, as we learn daily in other fields, may yield results that the most whole-hearted efforts fall short if misapplied. And the technique of the approach to poetry has not yet received half so much serious systematic study as the technique of pole-jumping. If it is easy to push up the general level of performance in such 'natural' activities as running or jumping . . . merely by making a little careful inquiry into the best methods, surely there is reason to expect that investigation into the technique of reading may have even happier results" (291–292). The invocation of "pole jumping" tells us that Richards had a precise understanding of technique. In the famous protocol experiment, he discovered that his students were failing at a basic level of technique: comprehension, or the technique of "construing." Conceding the objections raised to Richards's experiment, his analysis of technical failure appears to me confirmed by generations of teachers thereafter. Recognizing the difficulty of comprehending literary texts, a difficulty intrinsic to their literariness, was a necessary condition for the emergence of that technique we name now as close reading. Beyond the lecture hall, the condition of failure was a fact of reading as a mass

---

avant-garde, see Andreas Huyssen, *After the Great Divide* (New York: Palgrave Macmillan, 1987).

67. Richards, *Practical Criticism*, 297.

practice.[68] Richards was not training future literary critics to write literary criticism. The protocols were not intended as exercises in writing but as a means of *evincing* reading, of making it visible, and potentially capable of improvement.

Richards brought his technique of reading only so far as a propaedeutic, a therapeutic exercise. It was further developed and transmitted by his successors as a disciplinary mode of reading. And yet, it has been difficult to give this technique greater specificity in its dissemination than "attention to the words on the page." In this formulation, "attention" names a requisite for close reading, but no particular procedure of analysis. "Attention" here refers to the focus of the sensory and cognitive systems on a singular

68. Richards's identification of an array of interferences with reading, of which the "stock response" was representative, might be seen as a rearguard response to mass literacy, which is far more internally differentiated than polemics of the time suggest. It would require a separate (and potentially vast) inquiry to account for divergent modes of reading after the achievement of near-universal literacy, obviously not my purpose here. I mean only to suggest that it would be a mistake to dismiss Richards's response as simply reactive. It might be possible to update his terminology, for example, by translating notions such as "stock response" into information theory as the equivalent of "noise." Noise is present in every communication, at the least as the annunciator of the channel itself, the medium. In his famous protocol experiment, Richards attempted to foreclose noise by anonymizing the poems, but this strategy had the opposite effect of driving his readers to open the noisy channels of their response even wider, in a desperate attempt to find a ground for their impressions. Today we are disposed to acknowledge that noise can be recuperated as meaningful in interpretation, where it can appear in the guise of "ambiguity" (as in Empson's practice) or "context" (as with New Historicism and related methodologies). For a prescient effort to incorporate information theory into critical practice, see William R. Paulson, *The Noise of Culture: Literary Texts in a World of Information* (Ithaca, NY: Cornell University Press, 1988).

object. This heightened state indicates only the possibility of technique, not its actualization. I shall comment at the end of this essay on the question of attention; the question of minimal formality raises a more immediate theoretical problem. We will have to give an account of this feature if, as I propose, it was just this aspect of the technique that ensured its survival beyond the hegemony of the New Criticism. In fact, close reading had to be recollected in later decades as a technique far more rigidly prescribed than it actually was *in order to repudiate it*.

It will be helpful to approach the question of close reading as technique by way of a later attempt to pin it down to an itemized prescription. I cite here Vincent Leitch's effort in his *American Literary Criticism from the Thirties to the Eighties*, published in 1988:

In performing a close reading, a New Critic would generally:
(1) select a short text, often a metaphysical or modern poem;
(2) rule out "genetic" critical approaches;
(3) avoid "receptionist" inquiry;
(4) assume the text to be an autonomous, ahistorical, spatial object;
(5) presuppose the text to be *both* intricate and complex *and* efficient and unified;
(6) carry out multiple retrospective readings;
(7) conceive each text as a drama of conflicting forces;
(8) focus continually on the text and its manifold semantic and rhetorical interrelations;
(9) insist on the fundamentally metaphorical and therefore miraculous powers of literary language;

(10) eschew paraphrase and summary or make clear
that such statements are not equivalent to poetic
meaning;

(11) seek an overall balanced or unified comprehensive
structure of harmonized textual elements;

(12) subordinate incongruities and conflicts;

(13) see paradox, ambiguity, and irony as subduing
divergences and insuring unifying structure;

(14) treat (intrinsic) meaning as just one element of
structure;

(15) note in passing cognitive, experiential dimensions
of the text; and

(16) try to be the ideal reader and create the one, true
reading, which subsumes multiple readings.[69]

Leitch's checklist is suffused with an irony meant to relegate close reading to a pretheoretical past. The sixteen prescriptive items follow closely the method of Cleanth Brooks in *The Well Wrought Urn*, combined with the principles articulated by W. K. Wimsatt and Monroe Beardsley in their unavoidable essays on the "intentional" and "affective" fallacies. To what extent did the protocols Leitch enumerates actually dominate critical practice in the heyday of the New Criticism?

69. Vincent Leitch, *American Criticism from the Thirties to the Eighties* (New York: Columbia University Press, 1988), 35. In a later work, *Literary Criticism in the 21st Century: Theory Renaissance* (London: Bloomsbury, 2014), Leitch reduces his list from sixteen to ten items (39). He also pushes back against the reaffirmation of close reading, which he sees as implying a repudiation of theory and cultural studies (40–41).

In Leitch's account, a close reading is performed according to a set of rules—and quite a few of them! But we stumble already on the first of these rules. It is likely that the new technique of reading literary works would scarcely have endured had it been restricted to the reading of the "metaphysical or modern poem." In *The Well Wrought Urn*, Brooks tries to preempt the perception of limited application by extending his method to poems from all the major periods of English literature (the tactic also of *Understanding Poetry*). Had this extension failed, close reading would have disappeared quickly from the critical scene. I will not address most of the other items on Leitch's list except to suggest that these injunctions might or might not govern subsequent exercises in New Critical reading, and further, that the force of these injunctions weakened in succeeding decades.

There is one feature of close reading, however, only implicit in Leitch's recipe, that is worth singling out for its enduring effects, and that is the modeling function of the lyric poem. If the concept of the "poem" circulated in New Critical theory as a metonym for literature, it paradoxically authorized the extension of close reading to other forms of literature by constructing passages from these works as ontologically *like* poems.[70] This was perhaps a questionable construction, but it helped to establish literature as a defined object within the evolving disciplinary system by grounding the ontology of literature in its presumptively most prestigious form. The tactic of analogizing all literary works to

70. In the case of lyric poems themselves, as Leitch observes, the poem was often analogized to a drama. The prevalence of this tactic suggests that the point was in part the analogy itself, which jolted reading into a higher state of attention by dislocating the generic frame.

poems had surprising curricular consequences: it paradoxically secured the place of novels as canonical literary works
and objects worthy of close textual study. The New Criticism
launched thousands of "readings" of novels by way of reading passages from them. How many interpretations of James,
Melville, Woolf, and so many others were produced in the
postwar period, all generated by close reading of passages?
Close reading vastly increased the productivity of scholarship; that effect was enabled not by its programmatic features
so much as by its minimal formality, signaled by its approach
to any literary work, or even any passage from that work, as
like its approach to the lyric poem.[71]

If close reading succeeded as a relatively informal technique, we might begin to isolate its disseminated form by
paring away most of the items enumerated by Leitch. What
remains? I will attempt to characterize this remainder by recalling an argument advanced by W. K. Wimsatt in an essay
entitled "Explication as Criticism," delivered at the English
Institute proceedings of 1951.[72] Attempting to define a technique of reading prevalent among his New Critical peers,
Wimsatt identifies this practice at first as "explication," a
word that suggests a mode of reading that is relatively mod-
est by comparison to what we usually mean by interpretation. The fact that Wimsatt draws an implicit distinction
between explication and the more elaborated practice of

71. I note here a relatively unexplored theoretical problem related to the
function of the quoted passage in the close reading of prose works. Passages
obviously have a synecdochic function in this context, but they also constitute
quasi-unities in themselves, inviting formal analogy to a lyric poem.

72. W. K. Wimsatt, "Explication as Criticism," in *Explication as Criticism:
Selected Papers from the English Institute, 1941–1952*, ed. W. K. Wimsatt, Jr.
(New York: Columbia University Press, 1963), 2–26.

interpretation seems to me crucial, justifying my hypothesis that close reading was indeed a minimalist technique. But the word "explication," as a possible name for this practice, presents Wimsatt with difficulties, first of all the problem of the relation between explication and *judgment*, or criticism as it was traditionally defined. This is not the question, Wimsatt writes, of "whether it is necessary to understand a poem in order to criticize it"—this is too obvious to need demonstration—but the more puzzling problem of "whether to understand a poem is the same as to criticize it" (1). Richards, we recall, was confident that "comprehension" did indeed do most of the work of judgment, but Wimsatt wants to submit this assumption to scrutiny.[73] Writing two decades on from *Practical Criticism*, Wimsatt surveys the critical field and wonders, with surprise, why no one has offered to describe or define the technique that seemed somehow to enact a judgment of the work in the very process of expressing an understanding of it. Interestingly, Wimsatt does not advert to the concept of "close reading." Is the proper name of this technique, then, "explication"? Well, not quite.

"Explication," as Wimsatt employs this term, is more or less equivalent to Richards's sense of "comprehension," the construing of meaning at the level of words, phrases, lines, and sentences that might then be scaled up to the whole work. Explication's domain of practice raises the further question of relation to its French cognate, *explication de texte*, which Wimsatt worriedly considers: "It is not clear to me, indeed, that Dryden, in providing a motto

---

73. Richards, *Practical Criticism*: "good reading, in the end, is the whole secret of 'good judgment'" (287).

for the organ of our guild—'The last verse is not yet suffi-
ciently explicated'—had in mind more than the explication
of the explicit. But the explicator will surely not conceive
that he has employed his talent unless he performs not only
that service (as in glosses and other linguistic and historical
observations) but also the explicitation of the implicit. For
poetry is never, or even mainly, 'poetry of statement'" (3).
If explication means bringing a certain amount of learning
to our reading of a literary text, this does not, in Wimsatt's
view, constitute an act of criticism. Thus far, he is saying
nothing more than what Brooks contended in his polemic
against "paraphrase," the equivalent of what Wimsatt cites
as "poetry of statement." Wimsatt goes on, then, to disam-
biguate explication from *explication de texte* ("glosses and
other linguistic and historical observations") by introducing
a variant concept: *explicitation*. The novel concept of "explicitation" hints more emphatically at a *process* of reading,
an effort to make this process more visible. A further distinction between the "explicit" and the "implicit"—"those two
sides of the explicable"—aims to grasp a technique of reading that in its very process implies an act of judgment, what
Wimsatt calls "evaluation through explication" (3). I have
already suggested that the new technique of reading did indeed routinely perform this function. It is possible now to
demonstrate how this happens, even while observing that
this judicial function lapsed over time.

Having asserted the performative identity of explicitation and judgment, Wimsatt offers a theoretical argument in
support of that equation: "any theory of poetry" will regard
"the poem as an organized whole—a wholeness of vision, that
is, established through wholeness of diverse, but reconciled,
parts" (2). The process of explicitating brings out the relation

of the part to the whole, an implicit relation that does not wait for an interpretation of the whole work in order to impute meaning to elements of the text, that is, to comprehend these elements. It is the very possibility of explicitating the trajectory from a part to the whole that confirms the literary work *as* a whole.

Wimsatt's holistic language, enacting a version of the "hermeneutic circle," sounds archaic to our ears. It represents an effort to force a theoretical break with the hegemony of historical scholarship, which is demoted to the "explication of the explicit," the technique extending back from *explication de texte* to its ancient origins in the commentary tradition.[74] That technique was once content with explicating small segments of text, without positing an interpretation of the whole work (though such an interpretation was not excluded). In order to see where the alternative technique of explicitation leads, it will be necessary to wrest Wimsatt's notion from his theoretical holism. This holism falls right away into a quandary, because, as Wimsatt acknowledges, literary works can manifest aspects of holistic integrity at virtually every level— from phrases to lines of poetry, to stanzas, paragraphs, scenes or acts in dramas, chapters in novels, and so forth. These terms name conventional structural divisions, and they can exhibit unities of various kinds; but they are not the only structures that constitute resonant meanings that can be "explicitated" in the technique Wimsatt projects. These other resonant features have no name; neither are they necessarily coterminous with the work. They might govern portions of text smaller

74. René Wellek confirms the distinction in "The New Criticism: Pro and Contra," *Critical Inquiry* 4.4 (Summer 1978): "it is a mistake to consider close reading a new version of *explication de texte*" (620).

than the work or larger, on up to oeuvres and genres. Later, they will be recognized as *networks* or *patterns* of words, images, themes, syntactic structures, figures, descriptive details, narrative scenarios . . . the possibilities are innumerable.

Wimsatt's holism, like the organicism of the New Critics generally, compelled him to identify the connections he discerned between "parts" of a work as evidence of the unity of the work; but this was an unnecessary hypothesis. Close reading eventually liberated itself from the fetishization of the organic whole, a process that coincided with the recession of the lyric poem as the model object of criticism. Critics later find Wimsatt's implicit relations wherever they look for them—not surprisingly, because networks really exist and traverse literature at every level from individual works to oeuvres to genres to massive textual corpora. Versions of this quest for resonant singularities will support the vast productivity of literary criticism in the decades to follow, up to and including the patterns detected by data-mining programs.[75]

75. Patterns in texts do not interpret themselves, even when the observation of pattern sets out from the work of close reading. For a discussion of "pattern recognition" across the span from close reading to digital analysis, see Hoyt Long and Richard Jean So, "Literary Pattern Recognition: Modernism between Close Reading and Machine Learning," *Critical Inquiry* 42.2 (Winter 2016): 235–267. See also Ted Underwood, *Distant Horizons: Digital Evidence and Literary Change* (Chicago: University of Chicago Press, 2019): "Moreover, quantitative models still have to be interpreted, and the interpretation of literary models will depend to some extent on attentive reading of particular works and passages" (209). The distinction between "close" and "distant" reading has often been correlated with the distinction between qualitative and quantitative, but this is an imperfect alignment. Quantitative analysis can be undertaken for individual works, even very brief poems or short stories. It functions in these contexts *as* close reading. An early example of such a technique was developed by Edith Rickert in her nearly forgotten *New Methods for the Study*

If the New Critics' metaphysical belief in organic unity became more or less optional, and later even an embarrassment, the core procedure Wimsatt describes as "explicitation" became the practical basis for raising reading to a new level of technique. Explicitation is not interpretation, but the name for a technique of reading that makes *an account of the reading process the basis for interpretation*. Very simply, explicitation is a showing of the work of reading.[76] It puts pressure on the moment of reading when the comprehension of a text's elemental features turns, or struggles to turn, toward the correlation of those features with larger structures of meaning. The explicitation of what is implicit constitutes an infrastructure for interpretation. This structure is exposed, in the way that modernist architects expose the infrastructure of their buildings. In practical terms, this means that close reading can be exhibited, that it is not identical only to the solitary exercise of reading carefully or slowly.

Close reading, then, does not imply any particular mode of interpretation or grander agenda of criticism. The hermeneutic tradition, with all its interpretive schemes, flows

_____

of Literature (Chicago: University of Chicago Press, 1927). Her work has been happily brought back into the history of criticism by Buurma and Heffernan, *The Teaching Archive*, 88–106. For an inquiry into early quantitative criticism, see Yohei Igarashi, "Statistical Analysis at the Birth of Close Reading," *New Literary History* 46.3 (Summer 2015): 485–504.

76. This borrowing from mathematics gestures toward the technicity of close reading, which, as we have seen, struck its contemporaries at first as an imitation of scientific method. Close readings are not, of course, "proofs" in the mathematical or scientific sense, but exhibitions of a methodical mode of reading. Anirudh Sridhar, Mir Ali Hosseini, and Derek Attridge, eds., *The Work of Reading: Literary Criticism in the 21st Century* (Cham, Switz.: Palgrave Macmillan, 2021), gestures in its title to the direction pursued here. For other examples of this phrase in recent use, see Newstok "Archive."

like a jet stream far above close reading's groundwork.[77] For this reason, close readings of a text can yield different and even contradictory interpretations.[78] This is sometimes difficult to see, because in the writing of criticism, showing the work of reading can be integrated almost seamlessly into interpretive argument. The emphasis must be placed, however, on the qualifier *almost*: the work of reading has to remain visible within interpretation, as its provocation; otherwise, the performative impact of close reading will be blunted and its evidentiary value lost. Conversely, close reading does not guarantee validity in interpretation; rather, it opens interpretation to inspection and contestation by other readers.

We might be tempted to say of "showing the work of reading," "Is that all?" Yes, that *is* all. I will go further and

77. An early example: Johann Gottfried Herder's essay of 1773, *Shakespeare*, trans. Gregory Moore (Princeton, NJ: Princeton University Press, 2008), a founding document in the history of hermeneutics, contains no close textual analysis at all.

78. The same fluidity obtains for the expression of style in close reading, its capacity to enable individuating writing effects. Close reading as technique served the idiosyncratic style of Empson just as well as it served the impersonal style of Wimsatt. On the relation between close reading and style, see D. A. Miller, *Jane Austen, or The Secret of Style* (Princeton, NJ: Princeton University Press, 2003), 57–58. Miller sees the relation between the narrator and the character whose thoughts are disclosed in free indirect style as restaging a contradiction in the close reader's relation to the text: on the one hand, a bid for mastery over the text, even to the point of overwriting it with the reader's own words, and on the other, a self-abjecting submission to the words of the text. Miller's meditation on the closeness of close reading opens the trope to senses not demanded by the ordinary practice of disciplinary reading, but not excluded by it either. For further discussion of this issue, see Frances Ferguson, "Now It's Personal: D. A. Miller and Too-Close Reading," *Critical Inquiry* 41.3 (Spring 2015): 521–540.

say that literary scholars already know what close reading is—that it is just the procedure I describe. I have added nothing to that practical knowledge. But when we come to conceptualize close reading, to define it, we feel compelled to burden it with unnecessary descriptors and qualifications as well as ideological entailments. With regard to the last-named, close reading as a technique has no ideological or political implications whatsoever. This conclusion follows from the very nature of technique. A technique such as riding a bicycle or swimming—like reading itself—has no political implication *as technique*. On the other hand, the *distribution* of techniques almost always has political causes and consequences, perhaps none more significant historically than the distribution of literacy. Close reading, as an art cultivated by a fraction of the college-educated population, is unequally distributed too. Unfortunately, the distinction between technique and its political context has perplexed the history of close reading since its inception, a confusion it should be possible now to clarify.[79] At the least, we might argue that better

79. For some historians of the discipline, the political commitments of several New Critics—unquestionably racist and stridently anticommunist—are inextricable from the technique of close reading and are transmitted along with that technique. For a recent version of this argument, see Andy Hines, *Outside Literary Studies: Black Criticism and the University* (Chicago: University of Chicago Press, 2022). Hines is right about the political convictions of some New Critics, and he is also right that these beliefs may be implicit in their interpretations of literary works. I have made a similar argument in earlier work on conservative structures of thought in New Critical interpretations such as those in Brooks's *The Well Wrought Urn*. See *Cultural Capital: The Problem of Literary Canon Formation* (Chicago: University of Chicago Press, 1993), 134–175. For a nuanced account of New Critical political positions, see Mark Jancovich, *The Cultural Politics of the New Criticism* (Cambridge: Cambridge University Press, 1993). Jancovich is interested particularly

close reading serves the purpose of critique, and that it would be unwise to deprive critique of this tool.

We find it difficult to believe that close reading is so minimal a procedure as I am proposing here, not because we do not know how to do it, but because we misunderstand its nature as technique. We misunderstand the constitutive minimalism of technique. At the same time, "showing the work of reading" is more than paying attention to the words on the page. Close reading is a minimal but not a simple procedure. At the least, close reading requires reflection—or, to employ

─────

in the anticapitalism of the first generation of New Critics—Ransom, Tate, and Warren. This position owed much, of course, to the romantic medievalism of T. S. Eliot and Ezra Pound. The New Critics' critique of industrial capitalism might be read out of context as surprisingly progressive, though it was based on an agrarianism uncritical of its implication in the racism of the US South. (Warren repudiated his earlier position on race in later writing.) Granted the facts of this history, it is worth recalling that the spectrum of political opinion among the larger group of Anglo-American close readers was diverse. The reactionary views of Ransom, Tate, Wimsatt, and the early Warren were not congruent with those of Richards, Leavis, Empson, or Burke, all of whom occupied leftist or liberal positions on the political spectrum of their time. For a judicious effort to situate the American New Critics politically, see Louis Menand, *The Free World: Art and Thought in the Cold War* (New York: Farrar, Straus and Giroux, 2021), 461–474. The political indeterminacy of close reading is interestingly confirmed by the famous case of James Jesus Angleton, a fanatical anticommunist and high-ranking CIA officer who was taught by the New Critics at Yale in the 1940s. It has been easy to invoke Angleton's induction into close reading as evidence of the intrinsically reactionary politics of the technique itself. But this assumption is not borne out by the actual practice of the intelligence agencies, as described by the historian Michael Holzman in *Spies and Traitors: Kim Philby, James Angleton and the Friendship and Betrayal that Would Shape MI6, the CIA and the Cold War* (New York: Pegasus Books, 2021): "Angleton had been taught close reading at Yale. OSS, and MI-6, would teach him to read all over again. Interestingly, the kind of student he became was that specifically discouraged by his Yale teachers: he became a student of the history and contemporary context of the texts he studied" (87). The methodology Holzman describes is closer to New Historicism than to New Criticism.

the language of systems theory, a "second order observation." In close reading, we observe not only the text but our observation of the text. Although such reflection need not extend beyond the scene of thought, it is always capable of being exhibited in oral or written forms of expression, making the work of reading visible to others.[80]

Despite its minimalism, close reading was enough of a game changer to consolidate the diverse modes of literary criticism into a discipline with a core practice that straddled the classroom and the writing of the critical essay.[81] Explicitation was a new enough game to become on occasion an end in itself. These autotelic occasions are likely now to be seen as largely those of the classroom. Stand-alone close readings are difficult to justify in print, however virtuosic they may be. Interpretation remains the higher stake.[82] And yet, the appeal

---

80. I differ in this formulation from Jonathan Kramnick's argument in *Criticism and Truth* that close reading is a craft exclusively of writing. This restriction leaves us with the problem of how to characterize the cognitive work that goes into reading before the critic begins to write. In addition, many critics do not write or publish for long periods of time, perhaps most of their career; the work of reading for them goes into their teaching, or into conversation with other scholars. My sense is that much of what Kramnick wants to say about the craft of criticism can stand without the restriction to writing.

81. In *The Resistance to Theory* (Minneapolis: University of Minnesota Press, 1986), Paul de Man gives an accurate description of the New Critical version of close reading in his account of Reuben Brower's classroom procedure of the 1950s: "They [the students] were asked, in other words, to begin by reading texts closely as texts and not to move at once into the general context of human experience or history. Much more humbly or modestly, they were to start out from the bafflement that such singular turns of tone, phrase, and figure were bound to produce in readers attentive enough to notice them" (23).

82. The emergence of close reading as a disciplinary practice during the interwar period does not mean that the technique had never been employed before then. The "crux" in textual editing often provoked close reading, a

of the technique was powerful enough to permit any particular interpretation of a literary work after the New Criticism to offer itself as a "reading" of that work.[83] The metonym is the signal of technique. Not surprisingly, the generativity of close reading became increasingly problematic in the postwar period. A little close reading goes a long way; a lot risks tedium, which was not always avoided in the postwar decades.[84]

Explicitation became the everyday business of criticism.[85] Neither Wimsatt nor Brooks would have contemplated so

---

precedent frequently cited by Empson in *Seven Types of Ambiguity*. On Empson's use of textual criticism, see Thaventhiran, *Radical Empiricists*, 92–122. Translation produces similar kinds of textual crux, although the work of reading has to be retro-engineered in this context from the translation itself. Showing the work of reading has other precedents in the history of literary pedagogy—for example, the scene recorded by Coleridge in the *Biographia Literaria* of his childhood teacher, the Reverend James Bowyer, who liked to say that in a great poem there is a reason "not only for every word, but for the position of every word." See Samuel Taylor Coleridge, *Biographia Literaria*, ed. J. Shawcross (Oxford: Oxford University Press, 1907), 1:4–5. This passage is cited as a precedent to close reading in Brower, *In Defense of Reading*, 6–7.

83. When close reading is pressed to serve *as* interpretation, it sometimes yields an argument that interprets the literary work as about itself. New Criticism exploited this circularity of the reading-interpretation relation on many occasions; it was a specialty of Brooks, exemplified in his figure of the "well wrought urn." Paul de Man famously elaborated the strategy into an "allegory of reading" that emerges from the collapse of interpretation onto the moment of failed comprehension, the failure of reading. Close reading in this mode traps meaning in a cul-de-sac, yielding the same interpretation ultimately for every literary work; every work becomes an "allegory of reading."

84. See T. S. Eliot's well-known complaint about the "lemon-squeezer school of criticism" in "The Frontiers of Criticism," *The Sewanee Review* 64.4 (October–December 1956): 537.

85. It would be a mistake, however, to see close reading as the *only* business of criticism after its dissemination in the 1940s. In addition to the "business as usual" that was literary history—still the greater measure of published

vulgar a description of their technique as that implied by the term "business," but one of their peers, John Crowe Ransom, invoked just this notion in the title of his most important essay, "Criticism, Inc." Although Ransom apologizes for resorting to this possibly "distasteful figure," he saw more clearly than other New Critics what it meant for criticism to be grounded in a technique of reading. He understood that what was implicit in the technique was *productivity*, a way of revaluing the labor of the critics as a technical proficiency: "Rather than occasional criticism by amateurs, I should think the whole enterprise might be seriously taken in hand by professionals."[86] This famous sentence is preceded by two notable paragraphs that clarify the disciplinary stakes of technique:

> Criticism must become more scientific, or precise and systematic, and this means that it must be developed by the

---

scholarship—at least one other mode of criticism ought to be acknowledged as a competitor to close reading: genre criticism. This mode of interpretation was espoused by the Chicago School of Aristotelian criticism, which contended with New Criticism—in the end, unsuccessfully—for hegemony in this period. A different version of genre criticism achieved prominence in Frye's *Anatomy of Criticism*, which also briefly competed with New Critical hegemony before slipping into disfavor. For genre criticism, individual works serve to exemplify a particular genre, which in turn becomes the actual object of interpretation. This mode of criticism has shadowed close reading throughout its history, most consequentially in versions of Marxist criticism. In our own time, digital analysis has revived genre criticism, and with it the role of the text as example. Some of the difficulties in establishing a relation between close reading and distant reading follow from the strong reentry of genre into disciplinary practice.

86. John Crowe Ransom, *The World's Body* (New York: C. Scribner's Sons, 1938), 329.

collective and sustained effort of learned persons—which means that its proper seat is in the universities.

Scientific: but I do not think we need be afraid that criticism, trying to be a sort of science, will inevitably fail and give up in despair, or else fail without realizing it and enjoy some hollow and pretentious career. It will never be a very exact science, or even a nearly exact one. But neither will psychology, if that term continues to refer to psychic rather than physical phenomena; nor will sociology as Pareto, quite contrary to his intention, appears to have furnished us with evidence for believing; nor even will economics. It does not matter whether we call them sciences or just systematic studies; the total effort of each to be effective must be consolidated and kept going. The studies which I have mentioned have immeasurably improved in understanding since they were taken over by the universities, and the same career looks possible for criticism. (329)

Contemplating these words today, it is clear that Ransom is making an important statement, perhaps the greatest insight into his moment coming down to us. His contemporaries, however, saw his claim as pretentious, a confession of the mimetic scientism of the New Critics. Neither they nor possibly Ransom himself fully understood what was implied by the gesture toward the "scientific," though Ransom is obviously attempting to grasp the fact of technique. Having taken his insight a little too far, he starts to back away from the identification of criticism with science and keeps backing away till the end of the passage. The New Criticism, as a discourse seeking to produce knowledge about literature, was not by any measure a science, though it might have aspired to be "precise and systematic." The notion of "science" gestures toward something Ransom does not name in this passage, but which we can identify assuredly as technique.

Ransom was notable for his interest in technique, which he often identifies as the distinctive property of poetry; in this judgment, he is in accord with the fetish of the early New Critics. When he looks for technique, he finds it best exemplified in the most "technical" aspects of poetry, such as prosody:

> Studies in the technique of the art [of poetry] belong to criticism certainly. They cannot belong anywhere else, because the technique is not peculiar to any prose materials discoverable in the work of art, nor to anything else but the unique form of that art. A very large volume of studies is indicated by this classification. They would be technical studies of poetry, for instance, the art I am especially discussing, if they treated its metric; its inversions, solecisms, lapses from the prose norm of language, and from close prose logic; its tropes, its fictions, or inventions, by which it means to secure "aesthetic distance" and removes itself from history; or any other devices, on the general understanding that any systematic usage which does not hold good for prose is a poetic device. (347)

Technique can be invoked by tracing, as though with a transparency, the *techne* of poetry, its art (Ransom calls this "texture"). The critic engaged in "technical study" crawls across the page like an ant, taking inventory along the way of every "device" of poetic art. For Ransom, these devices distinguish poetry from prose, a dubious distinction when juxtaposed to the more inclusive concept of "literature," but serving the purpose here of modeling technique as such. Ransom describes a notionally pure technique, which literary critics seldom undertake to describe except possibly as an exercise. Such "technical study" risks tedium, like playing scales on a piano, technique that fails to ascend to a higher level of art. Here we return to the problem highlighted by Alan Brown earlier of the contradiction between technique and sensibility. This contradiction is highly resistant to theoretical resolution, but it is performatively overcome when "showing the work of reading" is successfully integrated into the construction of an interpretation, a higher level of art.[87]

The principle of minimal formality confirms the fact that close reading was not disseminated by prescription or recipe; rather, it was propagated by mutual imitation.[88] The muddle of practice that coalesced into New Criticism accounts for the two mistakes I have noted above: on the one hand, the failure to distinguish close reading from other techniques of reading closely, such as *explication de texte*; and on the other, the overspecification of close reading as a rigid prescription,

87. For a related sense of performance, see Peter Howarth, "Close Reading as Performance," in *Modernism and Close Reading*, ed. David James (Oxford: Oxford University Press, 2020), 45–68. Howarth sees the "performance" of close reading as extending the duration of the literary work as an "event" not completed until the reader engages with it. Howarth's "performance" rescues the literary object from the inert existence to which New Critical proscriptions of context seemed to condemn it.

88. Here is an example from Ransom, *The New Criticism* (Norfolk, CT: New Directions, 1941), of how this mutual imitation worked: "It does not seem impossible that we should obtain close studies of the structure-texture relations that poets have actually found serviceable in the past. The best endowed critic in the world for this purpose might well be, I should think, Mr. William Empson, the student of ambiguity" (275).

in the manner of Leitch's itemized account. Whatever else might be said about close reading—and that is quite a lot, a history yet to be written—the crucial point to be made about its historical emergence is that it was conspicuously more formal than the belletristic criticism that preceded it. Crossing the threshold of technique by explicitating the process of reading was sufficient to produce far-reaching effects, including the institutional effect of establishing criticism as a disciplinary practice distinct from literary history. In some respects, the emergence of close reading was an accident; but once it was devised as an imitable technique, its utility was indisputable. Its manifest and widespread appeal as technique explains why literary historians were forced to compromise with literary critics in the postwar decades of the twentieth century, to incorporate the new reading technique into normative scholarly practice.

I return once again and finally to the question with which I began: why the phrase "close reading" did not achieve consensus recognition until the 1960s. In the previous two decades the spatial trope had circulated intermittently, while the technique itself achieved the greatest extent of its dissemination, in both scholarship and teaching. The relatively small role of the term "close reading" as the name of the technique suggests that this mode of reading can be executed virtually without conceptualization. It is not necessary for those performing close reading to be able to give a precise verbal account of what they are doing, any more than it is necessary or even possible for musicians or athletes to give a precise verbal account of their performances. Minimal conceptualization of technique is compatible with a high level of artistry in performance. This muteness of technique is just as characteristic of a language art such as close reading as it is of any nonverbal art.[89] On this account, close reading is an "instrument" to the second order, analogous to techniques for playing a musical instrument such as a violin or piano. Close reading "plays" the literary work. An instrument does not determine what is played on it; nor does a basic technique for playing an instrument determine how well a piece of music will be performed. The instrument itself will always be just that; but the artistry with which the instrument is played has no determined outcome or limit of sophistication. This dual potentiality has indeed been our experience of close reading. It can be done in virtuoso fashion or as a mediocre exercise.

This analysis explains why it has been so difficult to define close reading, at the same time that it has been nearly impossible to supersede it. Minimal conceptualization is characteristic of close reading as technique.[90] It remains

89. This is the point of the second epigraph to this essay, drawn from the preface to Reuben Arthur Brower, *The Fields of Light: An Experiment in Critical Reading* (Oxford: Oxford University Press, 1951), a book that consists largely of close readings. Brower understands that when the technique of reading is performed well, it cannot be explained fully in terms other than those that compose the performance itself.

90. There are important implications here for the teaching of close reading, at both the undergraduate and the graduate levels. Teachers have often been frustrated by the difficulty of transmitting close reading as a foundational practice of criticism, as a consequence of which they look for a formula or recipe to guide its procedure. But transmission is much more likely to succeed if close reading is *modeled*, either in conversational exchange with students or by analysis of written examples (such as we find in Attridge and Staten, *The Craft of Poetry*). The teacher of close reading might be relieved of considerable anxiety by the recognition that, as in so much pedagogy immemorially, demonstration and imitation are much more effective as means of transmission than specifying a procedure precisely. The demonstrative modeling of close reading will likely produce diverse examples of procedure, depending on the text at hand, which is an entirely desirable result.

for us a stage—or, better, a *staging*—of reading, in advance of interpretation, taking the difficulty of the former as the occasion for the latter. The history of close reading is not the history of interpretation, then, such as we find in our ubiquitous theory manuals, according to which the New Criticism is one interpretive method—formalism—among many. The formalism so named is a set of interconnected hypotheses that define an ontology of the literary work of art. These hypotheses proved thereafter to be irrelevant to the function of close reading as technique. As we know, with the waning of the New Criticism, concepts derived from linguistics, anthropology, psychoanalysis, philosophy and other discourses entered Anglo-American literary study. Terms unknown to New Criticism supplemented the Brooksian trinity of irony, paradox, and ambiguity. The interpretive procedures that employed these new "theoretical" terms continued to invoke the metonym of "reading," all the way up to the algorithmic programs of distant reading, which disclose in massive textual corpora patterns of lexical and syntactic features that seem microscopic from the perspective of ordinary reading, even ordinary close reading. Although this technique looks like the most radical overthrow of close reading, it has been seen by some as its apotheosis.[91]

91. On this question, see Jin, "Problems of Scale." Jin analogizes "close" and "distant" in his argument to synecdoche and metonymy, or part-whole and part-part relations respectively. This is a useful way of grasping the scalability of both close and distant modes of reading, as opposed to the tendency to view close reading as dealing only with individual texts, distant reading only with massive numbers of texts. See also Katherine Bode, "The Equivalence of 'Close' and 'Distant' Reading; or, Toward a New Object for Data-Rich Literary History," *Modern Language Quarterly* 78 (2017): 77–106; and Jessica Pressman, *Digital Modernism: Making It New in New Media* (Oxford: Oxford University

Finally, because close reading entails no one mode of
interpretation for literary works, nothing prevents it (or
has prevented it) from articulation with historical or archi-
val scholarship. With a better understanding of this point,
literary study might finally move beyond the conflict between formalism and historicism that drags along so much
metaphysical and ideological baggage in its train. Extreme
oscillation between these theoretical poles is a sure indication of disciplinary crisis, such as we are passing through at
present.[92] Without inquiring further into the causes of what

---

Press, 2014). Pressman summarizes her position: "We need to recognize how
close reading is a historical and media-specific technique that, like other critical
practices, demands renovation as we embrace our modern age and its digital
literature" (18). On the other side of the argument, Matthew L. Jockers, in *Macroanalysis: Digital Methods and Literary History* (Urbana: University of Illinois
Press, 2013), argues strongly that close reading is inadequate as a method to sustain literary study into the future, and that it is time to make a definite transition
to distant reading—or "macroanalysis," to use his preferred term. Whatever distinction is asserted between close and distant reading, it is helpful to set out from
the recognition that the two are consonant as techniques. Beyond that ground
of identity, specifying their different technicities poses many theoretical problems, especially those arising from the difference in the scale of criticism's objects:
work, oeuvre, genre, corpus. Resolving issues of scale will no doubt also require
a better understanding of how meso-scale structures such as plot and character
are processed in the experience of reading. Other examples of meso-structure
would include the "clues" crucial to Franco Moretti's study of detective fiction.
The number of such structures is indeterminate, and they are peculiarly resistant
to reduction to the methodological techniques of either close reading or distant
reading. Of course, meso-structures are also in the end just assemblages of words,
but they are not processed cognitively in the same way that close reading does at
the scale of the quoted passage, or distant reading at the "bag of words" scale. For
an important retrospective on the theoretical questions raised by the technicities
of qualitative and quantitative modes of interpretation, see Franco Moretti, "The
Roads to Rome," *New Left Review* 124 (July–August 2020): 125–136.

92. Disciplinary crisis gave birth to close reading at an earlier moment of
oscillation between competing modes of reading, between the critics and the

seems to be a loss of faith in disciplinary modes of reading (these causes are both internal and external to the discipline), I propose that the reemergence of close reading in theoretical discourse has exposed the troubled border between disciplinary and lay practices of reading. In this context, it is precisely close reading's minimal formality that is of interest, the fact of its being located so near the threshold between the intuitive and the technical. This, I take it, is just the question raised by Derek Attridge and Henry Staten in their "minimal interpretation," which they might without apology embrace as an exemplary practice of close reading.

CODA: ON ATTENTION TO LITERATURE

There are other reasons for affirming close reading at the present moment that bring the notion of "attention to the words on the page" back into relation to the larger social frame of my argument. I have assumed throughout this book that attention is a necessary but not sufficient condition for establishing close reading as a cultural technique with (ordinarily) an institutional locus of practice. As a technique inaugurated by an act of attention, close reading is one of many possible attentional practices. In the university, some cultural disciplines employ parallel techniques of what we might call "close looking" and "close listening." Like close reading, these

---

literary historians. Crisis is not always the harbinger of disaster; it can be the occasion for resolution of long-standing problems in theory or practice.

techniques call for attention at the threshold of technique. This common feature of the cultural disciplines brings the larger social ecology of attention to the fore, as the environment of a cognitive state uniquely challenged by the cultural conditions of twentieth- and twenty-first-century modernity. No one needs to be persuaded that the demands on our attention emanating from new and old media are overwhelming; or that, conversely, *distraction* is the manic complement of attention—that we are, as T. S. Eliot famously declared in *Four Quartets*, "Distracted from distraction by distraction." "Attention" and "distraction" were favored terms for Eliot, Richards, and their contemporaries in their analyses of mass-mediated forms of culture. The declinist narratives so often resulting from these engagements, however, failed to account for the complexity of the psychological state indicated by the concept of attention. Every cultural work that distracts us does so by soliciting our attention. Attention and distraction are different expressions of the same cognitive complex, different ways of observing its operation.[93]

93. The subject of attention has occasioned a minor industry of commentary, usually taking as its point of departure William James's famous chapter on attention in his treatise of 1890, *The Principles of Psychology* (Cambridge, MA: Harvard University Press, 1981), 380–433. The phenomenon of distraction has correlatively been recognized as more than just the antithesis or failure of attention; it is rather a state that has its distinct occasions and pleasures. The complementarity of attention and distraction is explored at length by the art historian Jonathan Crary in *Suspensions of Perception: Attention, Spectacle, and Modern Culture* (Cambridge, MA: MIT Press, 1999), from which I cite this statement, summarizing psychological research: "the more one investigated, the more attention was shown to contain within itself the conditions for its own undoing—attention was in fact continuous with states of distraction, reverie, dissociation, and trance" (45–46).

Bearing this point in mind, it seems evident that the defense of literary reading against its rivals in the realm of cultural consumption too often resorts to a reductive emphasis on attention in an effort to save literature. If the immersive reading of long novels, for example, is offered as the chief case of failed attention among our students, it is easy to point to video gaming as a counterexample. This form has the effect of powerfully fixating attention, suggesting that attention alone is not the issue in the failure of literary reading. A better way to address this problem is to start from the difference between writing as a media form and the multimedia apparatus of the video game. The difference that matters is between writing's static marks on a page—the only source of visual stimulation the reading of a novel ordinarily affords—and the interactive kinetic imagery that is the vector of narrative in the video game. Narrative in written form can produce a kind of complex phenomenal experience that is available only in the medium of writing, where long strings of sentences generate singular effects of meaning.[94] This is not to deny that the video game—to stay with this example—delivers its own kind of complex narrative pleasure. It is rather to assert that the cognitive techniques demanded in the use of media as different as the novel and the video game are not easily commensurable and have to be socially valued separately. These two media forms are not just alternative vehicles for delivering narrative, the one more stimulating than the other in

94. The medial effect of writing cannot for this reason be represented predominantly by narrative, which is only one of many modes of writing. The writing effect as such belongs rather to the sheer concatenation of sentences, which results in a phenomenal experience unique to reading. The poverty of the visual stimulation afforded by lines of text contrasts greatly with the diverse forms of cognitive experience writing makes possible.

sensory terms. On the contrary, engagements with narrative in these two media are essentially different cognitive experiences. One cannot be substituted for the other.

As complementary states of mind, "attention" and "distraction" have been remarked for millennia. They constitute a primitive dialectic, operating at the level of the individual psyche but articulated to larger social structures. Was the Gothic cathedral, with its display of architectural and imagistic wonders, designed to focus attention on religious meaning or to distract the populace from its less stimulating everyday environment? Surely the one by means of the other. Every moment in which attention and distraction are set into relation by a technical artifact constitutes the experience of a modernity for a given population. These technological modernities go back very much farther than the interwar period of the twentieth century, when close reading was devised alongside the proliferation of film, radio, magazines, bestsellers—all the massified cultural forms provoking anxiety among the literary professoriate. Close reading emerged as a technique out of a paradoxical media situation in which the very forms of writing that could be regarded in earlier historical periods as sources of entertainment and therefore distraction—poems, novels, plays—were dialectically repositioned as demanding the most strenuous effort of attention.[95]

95. Nicholas Dames, in *The Physiology of the Novel: Reading, Neural Science, and the Form of Victorian Fiction* (Oxford: Oxford University Press, 2007), argues that distraction was solicited by the novel form itself. This thesis cautions us against positing the same attentional demand for all forms of writing. I do not mean to suggest, on the other hand, that literary works could not be read seriously or "closely" before the twentieth century; rather, these forms circulated in a cultural ecosystem in which the reading of scripture, devotional writing, and other moral or instructional genres was regarded as indisputably more serious

This new emphasis on attention to literature was not unjustified; it was a cultural development responding to the latest technological modernity, the diffusion of new media, along with the proliferation of writing itself in new popular as well as bureaucratic forms. The response was no doubt rhetorically overheated; but it was also the occasion for developing a technique of reading adjusted to a new condition of writing, and a new condition of literature. In that new condition, those literary works that successfully attracted close reading had the best chance to enter the school curriculum, and thus to survive over the long term.[96]

---

than the reading of poems, plays, and novels. Readers of Austen's *Pride and Prejudice* will recall the scene in which Mr. Collins is asked to read aloud from a novel to an assembled evening party. He replies scornfully that he does not read novels, and chooses instead to read several pages from Fordyce's *Sermons*. The lesson should be obvious for those of us who wonder how literature—even novels—can be regarded by some of our students with the same lack of relish as the iconic sermons of Fordyce. When teachers of literature confront resistance to the reading of long works such as novels, the problem is not so much the absolute inability of students to focus attention at all (that is a different question), but their experience (or lack of experience) with the medium of writing in certain of its generic forms. This is to say that attention is always oriented toward a particular object, and that the power of an object to actuate the attention/distraction complex is an index of its social condition.

96. For a fascinating study of how one poem—Thomas Wyatt's "They flee from me"—attracted iconic close reading by the New Critics, see Peter Murphy, *The Long Public Life of a Short Private Poem: Reading and Remembering Thomas Wyatt* (Stanford, CA: Stanford University Press, 2019), 175–209. In my experience, Wyatt's poem offers occasion for close reading in the classroom with its opening line, "They flee from me, that sometime did me seek." Who are "they"? *What* are "they"? Most students stumble over this threshold, a challenge to comprehension that conveniently opens a path for close reading. Other kinds of writing will suggest different paths to technique in close reading. Forging those paths for diverse works of literature has been a large part of post–New Critical literary study.

Literary scholars have not always been at ease with the fact that close reading functioned as a means of producing rarity in response to the condition of superabundant writing. Without question, close reading functioned as an institutional means of sorting literary work in the twentieth century and after, in response to the massification and potential ephemeralization of literary writing. Other institutions of sorting have emerged for this purpose too, such as the loose collection of agencies whose purpose is to award prizes. These agencies also produce rarity, improving the possibilities for circulation and preservation of prizewinning works.[97] The preeminent mechanism of sorting, however, remains the *market*, in which literary works are thrown into a pseudo-Darwinian competition for survival. There are reasons scholars might not want to cede the social function of sorting literary production wholly to the market. Close reading and distant reading are more allied in this purpose than we might suppose, in that they both constitute a nonmarket system of sorting. Distant reading works with the category of genre, for example, in order to bring the mass of writing into the domain of the intelligible, organized at the macro level by the distinction between "serious" and "popular" writing.[98]

97. The production of rarity is in turn subject to a reversal as the number of prize-awarding agencies increases and the number of prizewinning or "short-listed" works of literature accumulates beyond the ability of a single individual to read them. For an authoritative study of the prize-awarding system, see James English, *The Economy of Prestige: Prizes, Awards, and the Circulation of Cultural Value* (Cambridge, MA: Harvard University Press, 2008).

98. Franco Moretti and the Stanford Literary Lab offer a pioneering demonstration of this sorting effect in Mark Algee-Hewitt et al., "Canon/Archive," in *Canon/Archive: Studies in Quantitative Formalism*, ed. Franco Moretti (New York: n + 1 Books, 2017), 253–294. Taking as its object "type-

This sorting procedure delivers some literary works over to the procedure of close reading, although any and every literary work is in principle capable of being read closely, by one or another disciplinary technique.

In retrospect, close reading was destined to call forth its complement in distant reading, as the condition of reading and writing entered yet another phase of massification and technological disturbance. To put this proposition conversely, and also perhaps more precisely: Franco Moretti's call for "distant reading" in his 2000 essay, "Conjectures on World Literature," constructed distant reading as the properly dialectical complement of close reading.[99] When the implications

---

token" ratios in novels, this essay attempts to refind canonical works buried in the mass of the archive, to distinguish these works from the "great unread." My sense is that it will take some time to assess the implications of this project, which recovers a driver of canon-formation intrinsic to literary writing at the micro-level of style, something like the Holy Grail of distant reading.

99. The moment: Franco Moretti, "Conjectures on World Literature," *New Left Review* 54 (January–February 2000): 54–68, reprinted in *Distant Reading* (London: Verso, 2013): "At bottom [close reading is] a theological exercise—very solemn treatment of very few texts taken very seriously—whereas what we really need is a little pact with the devil: we know how to read texts, now let's learn how not to read them. Distant reading: where distance, let me repeat it, is a condition of knowledge" (48). My hypothesis of a dialectical moment is not the only way distant reading has been understood as historical. Ted Underwood, in "A Genealogy of Distant Reading," *Digital Humanities Quarterly* 11.2 (2017), http://www .digitalhumanities.org/dhq/vol/11/2/000317/000317.html, disassociates distant reading from new digital technology and discovers its origins in older scholarship such as that of Raymond Williams and Janice Radway, working "on the boundary between literary history and social science." Although I believe Underwood is right about the disciplinary foundations of distant reading (and he might not, in any case, reject the historical significance of Moretti's 2000 intervention), my story concerns the emergence of "distant reading" as a name that organizes practice in such a way as to evoke common features, and even to organize scholars into new

of distant reading began to sink into the consciousness of the literary professoriate, the dialectic of close and distant reading became inevitable. Moretti's invocation of distant reading, though it was not the first use of the term, was posed in such a way as to *create its moment*. Is it not evident in retrospect that our renewed interest in close reading today dates from this moment of distant reading's introduction? If we are dealing with a genuinely dialectical pivot in the discipline, it should no longer be possible to regard close reading and distant reading as procedures between which we must choose.

Refusing the undialectical choice also means recognizing that even the most sophisticated computational forms of distant reading cannot circulate as meaningful knowledge about the mass of literary writing if some portion of what is written is not read with immersive engagement or enhanced forms of attention—possibly even close reading. Returning to the conditions of close reading's emergence in the interwar period, I suggest that we might think of the technique at its origin as an effort to *deindustrialize* mass literacy, a notion that I offer here tentatively, and without (I hope) reintroducing a mode of cultural critique burdened with the metaphysical investments of the New Criticism.[100] These crypto-religious attach-

cadres. In this context, the term "distant reading" performs a disciplinary function analogous to that of "close reading."

100. *Deindustrialization*, because close reading orients the technique of reading toward a bodily *techne* (signaled by such tropes as "close" and "slow") and away from technology, which is inevitably associated in the social imaginary with machine manufacture. Perhaps this is why close reading, as typically practiced for most of its history, was indifferent to the technical medium, whether manuscript, print, or screen. Distant reading, by contrast, moves *toward* technology, toward computation by means of computer technology. For an account of what is implied by a media and technology-conscious relation

ments are recalled in Moretti's recognition of close reading as a "theological exercise," which perhaps leaves open the possibility of *detheologizing* the technique, purging it of its residual mystifications. In practice, this means opening the literary to the profane technique of quantitative analysis. Detheologizing does not imply an end to close reading, only the necessity of resituating it in the discipline.

The two imperatives of deindustrialization and detheologization punctuate the history of close reading, the record of the technique's struggle with the conditions of its emergence and reemergence. If this hypothesis is credible, it might explain close reading's return to the forefront of the discipline at the present moment, when digital technology has given us immeasurable new quantities of industrialized textual "content" and even the automation of writing itself.[101] The

to the literary object, see Alan Liu, *Friending the Past: The Sense of History in the Digital Age* (Chicago: University of Chicago Press, 2018); and Alan Liu, "Imagining the New Media Encounter," in *A Companion to Digital Literary Studies*, ed. Ray Siemens and Susan Schreibman (London: Wiley-Blackwell, 2008), 1–25.

101. Leroi-Gourhan did not foresee this development when he predicted the end of writing. Flusser, however, comes closer to envisioning the culmination of both reading and writing in total automation. See *Does Writing Have a Future?*: "This new way of reading is beginning to crystallize now. It is called, of course, 'computing'" (84). This kind of reading "no longer needs to be intelligent, to be about extracting meaning. It can concentrate on creative amalgamation" (85). The notion of "creative amalgamation" seems to prophesy ChatGPT. The procedure of a "large language model" is perhaps implicit in all writing; ChatGPT writes, as do humans, by assembling—"amalgamating"— what it reads. The margin of the creative in this amalgamation is yet to be determined. The tumultuous introduction of generative writing programs such as ChatGPT is only the latest episode in our never-ending struggle to understand what our technology does for us and to us. It will not be easy, for example, to establish a method to read the writing produced by our algorithmic

introduction of digital analysis into literary study forces us yet again to confront the question of what reading can be in an age of mass literacy, especially after that "mass" has been fractured into thousands of sites and modes of reading and writing, dispersed into what we now call "networks." If machine reading engages the massification of text production in order to produce knowledge about an otherwise unreadable accumulation, human reading will always be limited by the constraints of the human body; unlike machine reading, human reading is very slow indeed.[102] In the disciplinary form of close reading, reading is slowed down further still, in order for the reader to engage in a reflexive procedure of observing and manifesting the work of reading. Decelerating the pace of reading does not refer literally to the movement of the eyes across lines of text; the qualifier "slow" rather

---

programs. Can such writing be submitted to close reading? The fact that this writing is composed—or recomposed—of what human beings have already written does not immediately solve this problem. Yet N. Katherine Hayles is optimistic about a solution. See her "Afterword: Learning to Read AI Texts," *Critical Inquiry*, "Forum" (June 30, 2023), https://critinq.wordpress.com/2023/06/30/afterword-learning-to-read-ai-texts/.

102. Speed reading is a response to the same social conditions as close reading. Both techniques of reading—one a fraudulent commercial enterprise, the other an established method of reading situated in a university discipline—testify to the shock of mass literacy, the reader's expulsion from that (imaginary) pastoral scene in which there were fewer texts and more time to linger with these texts. Speed reading was never a solution to this problem, because the top speed of reading is a neurophysiological constant, determined by the minimum duration of saccades. No technique of human reading can exceed this speed limit, which is why techniques for human reading move in the opposite direction to technology, toward slowing reading down into a reflective process, an art.

signals the inauguration of technique, which requires time for reflection.[103]

We might see close reading today as the disciplinary analogue of the countercultural movement embracing "slow tech" and other slow forms of cultural consumption.[104] If the concept of attention announces this alternative mode of consumption in the instance of reading, it is also a name for what is problematic in our engagement with cultural works generally. Nothing ensures that our momentary attention to any particular cultural work, whatever its media form, will give us what we want from it—not unless we succeed in prolonging our attention, at least provisionally. In the course of this probationary engagement, we are sometimes able to arrest the constant deflections of our attention; we succeed in bringing our sensory and cognitive apparatuses into focus upon a single object, a neurophysiological state that distracts us from competing solicitations of attention. The ability to achieve this state has considerable social value, even if it is only sometimes achieved. Such coherent states of attention are difficult to produce and difficult to sustain. It is even

103. Harry Berger, Jr., argued for "decelerated" close reading in *Imaginary Audition: Shakespeare on Stage and Page* (Berkeley: University of California Press, 1989), 45, 144, 148, as did Sven Birkerts that same year in his "Note: Close Reading," in *The Electric Life: Essays on Modern Poetry* (New York: William Morrow, 1989), 92.

104. For an application of this value concept to the reading of literature, see David Mikics, *Slow Reading in a Hurried Age* (Cambridge, MA: Harvard University Press, 2013). For an overview, see Andrew Price, *Slow-Tech: Manifesto for an Over-Wound World* (London: Atlantic Books, 2009); and Rob Kitchin and Alistair Fraser, *Slow Computing: Why We Need Balanced Digital Lives* (Bristol: Bristol University Press, 2020).

more challenging to raise these attentive states to the level of technique, or *techne*.

Heretofore, we have been inclined to conceive of attention too simply in terms of an economy, as a quantum, usually measured as the time we devote to any particular object of attention.[105] But this construction does not do justice to the nature of attention as the condition for extremely diverse dispositions toward cultural artifacts, marked both by different commitments in time and by different modes of engagement. It is not surprising that this qualitative diversity characterizes our engagement with written artifacts, perhaps more than with most of the objects soliciting our attention. There are many ways to read. In this context, it is worth repeating that immersive reading is not close reading, and that close reading interrupts immersive reading in order to initiate a rarified technique. Let us also admit that the quality of attention demanded by the form of reading we call "close" is difficult to sustain outside an institutional setting, such as the discipline of literary study affords. Other kinds of reading closely, of course, have other social and institutional scenes of practice.[106]

The value of close reading as technique is more than great enough, in my view, to merit its continued support,

105. I follow the argument here (with some reservations) of Yves Citton, *The Ecology of Attention*, trans. Barnaby Norman (Cambridge: Polity Press, 2017). Citton wants to move away from the "economy of attention" to an "ecology," in which individual acts of attention are seen as "essentially *collective*" (7). Citton is building on as well as revising the earlier work of Richard Lanham, *The Economics of Attention: Style and Substance in the Age of Information* (Chicago: University of Chicago Press, 2006).

106. I have attempted a taxonomy of the modes of reading specific to scholarship in "How Scholars Read."

even if this art is for the most part confined to the university. There is no point in forcing close reading, as a modality of attentional practice, into competition with the alternative modes of reading described by N. Katherine Hayles as "hyper" and "distant."[107] The domain of close reading is necessarily circumscribed in relation to the diversity and multiplicity of reading situations. Attempting a balanced view of the current status of close reading in *The Ecology of Attention*, Yves Citton follows Hayles's taxonomy in urging this policy: "The humanities should adopt a PLURALIST UNDERSTANDING OF READING, recognizing the *complementary (rather than rival) nature of close reading, distant hyper-reading and machine reading*" (148). The recommendation is not unwarranted. There is no literary pedagogy as yet, however, that gives these modes of reading equal time in the classroom. The phenomenal diversity of reading argues against a pluralism in which modes are simply equated.[108] We might even want to concede the greater social value of immersive reading by comparison to all the modes addressed by Hayles and Citton. The ongoing legitimation crisis of literary study

107. N. Katherine Hayles, "How We Read: Close, Hyper, Machine" *ADE Bulletin* 150 (2010): 1–18.

108. To specify the conditions which a commensuration of reading modes would have to acknowledge: (1) *close reading* assumes a collectivity of university or college-educated readers, engaged with literary texts in the classroom or in scholarly writing; (2) *hyper reading* is something everyone does, both inside and outside the academy, as a largely intuitive action, though it might well be submitted to methodization; and (3) *machine reading* involves a highly technical specialization undertaken at present only by a fraction of the humanities professoriate and (as yet) imperfectly reconciled with earlier disciplinary norms. *Immersive reading* falls outside this taxonomy, as a practice mainly of the lay mode of reading, which can of course be undertaken by both lay and professional readers.

that employs the slogans of "surface reading" and "postcritique" testifies to an ongoing reevaluation of reading in the immersive form, as practiced by both professional and lay readers. Only this form ultimately secures the future of literature. Still, the disciplinary technique of close reading has an important role to play in response to a media situation revolutionized once again by new technology. The least that one might say about the social importance of close reading is that, as one technique of reading among others, it is a node in a larger, unorganized network of attentional techniques, both within and without the university. These cultural techniques are well worth the effort of their transmission.

ANNOTATED BIBLIOGRAPHY

Scott Newstok

BOSWELL: Then, Sir, what is poetry?
JOHNSON: Why Sir, it is much easier to say
what it is not. We all *know* what light is;
but it is not easy to *tell* what it is.

JAMES BOSWELL,
Life of Samuel Johnson (1791)

single phrases
. . . contain a whole library of meanings

EDWARD SAID, "Erich Auerbach,
Critic of the Earthly World" (2004)

This bibliography documents some key moments in the still-unfolding history of close reading, from its tentative origins to the recent flood of scholarship on the subject.[1] Thematic clusters generally correspond to decades across the last century, but I've ranged at will as needed.

This print list gleans from the more substantial online archive I've compiled at **www.closereadingarchive.org**. That archive preserves far more text than this reduced print version permits (indeed, the former exceeds the latter by a factor of fifty). Beyond its extensive scope, the online archive excerpts passages from the entries, which are often revelatory (if sometimes oppressive in their repetitiousness!).

Yet even brief mentions of "close reading" in passing prove to be edifying; in aggregate, the archive corroborates that the phrase has remained in contentious circulation for nearly a century. Until recent decades, most of the significant statements in this history appear in publications that don't overtly announce "close reading" in their titles. A few examples: "the method of close reading" was first invoked in a 1946 essay on Coleridge by Howard Hall Creed; "the practice of close

---

1. For a quick index of this surge, here's the tally of the phrase "close reading" appearing in titles cataloged by Google Scholar, (roughly) tripling in each decade following the 1970s:

1950s: 1
1960s: 14
1970s: 16
1980s: 42
1990s: 119
2000s: 282
2010s: 978

reading," in a 1956 biographical entry on John Crowe Ransom by Edwin Harrison Cady et al.; and "the theory of close reading," in a 1979 book titled *The Interpretation of Otherness* by Giles Gunn. The archive thus recovers a tacit discourse that is happening in, below, and through all sorts of other arguments. Constructed on the principle of quotation rather than narration, it surfaces a new history of the discipline.

If the following selection entices you to explore the online archive, you might find yourself surprised by the sheer volume of writing on this topic, which has steadily increased since the 1970s, apparently unaffected by shifting disciplinary tides. Patterns begin to emerge: early comments about close reading tend to stem from outside the university, while contemporary scholars increasingly attempt to establish the genealogy of the practice. Searching permits you to gather your own harvest—whether all of a critic's discussions of "close reading," an anthology of poems, or even a painting. May my choices in this bibliography be the foil to the hidden pearls you find in the archive.

In this book, many questions are inevitably opened up yet not pursued, much less resolved. Even an abbreviated record of efforts to define close reading underscores the key query of Guillory's essay: *why is it so difficult to articulate what many in the discipline take to be its central practice?* The manifold occasions of these efforts cumulatively confirm that "close reading" focalizes anxieties beyond the "mere" technique of reading a literary text.

This bibliography's chronology itself tells a story, one that can only be hinted at in print. Perhaps those who survey the archive will assemble their own alternative accounts—so much the better.

"The word is late, but the thing is auncient"[2]

In the spirit of *préfiguration retroactive*,[3] contemporary scholars have suggested numerous forerunners of what we now call "close reading" that appeared long before the professional practice was consolidated in the early twentieth century; some seek precedents "at least as far back as Quintilian and Cicero."[4] Nelson annexes Torquato Tasso's 1594 *Discourses on the Heroic Poem* as a humanist instance (120); McLane points to Joseph Ritson's 1794 "Historical Essay on Scottish Song" (257); Selbin adduces John Cassell's 1850s periodicals (494); Morgan summons Vernon Lee's 1913 *The Beautiful: An Introduction to Psychological Aesthetics* (51). Among the scores of other antecedents that have been proffered are Longinus's *On the Sublime*; the Second Sophistic movement; Origen's *Homilies on Genesis and Exodus*; Rufinus of Aquileia's translation of Eusebius; medieval grammarians; Lorenzo Valla's 1440 *Discourse on the Forgery of the Alleged Donation of Constantine*; Desiderius Erasmus's 1516 *Methodus*; Michel de Montaigne's

---

2. Francis Bacon, unpublished draft of the dedication to Prince Henry for the second edition of the *Essayes or Counsels, Civill and Moral* (c. 1610–12); British Library, MS Additional 4259, fol. 155.

3. Henri-Louis Bergson, *La pensée et le mouvant* (1934 ed.), 23–24, as cited in Quian Zhongshu, *Patchwork: Seven Essays on Art and Literature* (Leiden: Brill, 2014), 31 n. 4.

4. Russ McDonald, Nicholas D. Nace, and Travis D. Williams, eds., "Introduction," in *Shakespeare Up Close: Reading Early Modern English Texts* (London: Bloomsbury, 2013), xxiii.

1580–1595 *Essays*; George Puttenham's 1589 *Arte of English Poesie*; Thomas Hobbes's 1620 *Discourse upon the Beginning of Tacitus*; John Donne's 1620s sermons; John Dryden's 1668 *Essay of Dramatick Poesie*; responses to Pope's 1715–1720 translation of *The Iliad*; William Warburton's 1740 *A Vindication of Mr. Pope's Essay on Man*; Robert Lowth's 1753 *Lectures on the Sacred Poetry of the Hebrews*; Samuel Johnson's 1779–1781 *Lives of the Most Eminent English Poets*; Hugh Blair's 1783 *Lectures on Rhetoric and Belles Lettres*; Johann Wolfgang von Goethe's 1815 *Proverbs*; Samuel Taylor Coleridge's 1817 *Biographia Literaria*; R. J. Mann's 1856 *"Maud" Vindicated*; Gerard Manley Hopkins's 1862 notebooks; John Ruskin's 1865 *Sesame and Lilies*; Friedrich Nietzsche's 1881 *Daybreak*; James Lane Allen's 1883 "On the First Page of *The Portrait of a Lady*"; Alexander Bain's 1887 *On Teaching English*; Oscar Wilde's 1889 "The Portrait of Mr. W. H."; Francis H. Stoddard's 1892 "Technique in Emily Dickinson's Poems"; and W. E. B. Du Bois's 1903 *The Souls of Black Folk*. Hancher has searched for early English instances of "close" (and its synonyms) occurring near "reading" (and its synonyms), turning up attestations dating back to William Cave's 1673 *Primitive Christianity*.

1992:   Lowry Nelson, Jr., "Close Reading of Lyric Poetry," in *Poetic Configurations: Essays in Literary History and Criticism* (University Park, PA: Penn State University Press), 115–125.

2010:   Maureen N. McLane, "Mediating Antiquarians in Britain, 1760–1830: The Invention of Oral Tradition; or, Close Reading before Coleridge," in *This Is Enlightenment*, ed. Clifford Siskin and William Warner (Chicago: University of Chicago Press), 247–264.

2012:   Benjamin Morgan, "Critical Empathy: Vernon Lee's
        Aesthetics and the Origins of Close Reading," *Victorian
        Studies* 55.1 (Autumn): 31–56.

2016:   Michael Hancher, "Re: Search and Close Reading," in *De-
        bates in the Digital Humanities* (Minneapolis: University
        of Minnesota Press), 118–138.

2016:   Jesse Cordes Selbin, "'Read with Attention': John Cassell,
        John Ruskin, and the History of Close Reading," *Victo-
        rian Studies* 58.3 (Spring): 493–521.

"All respectable poetry invites close reading"

While some have alleged that "Richards' assertion that 'all
respectable poetry invites close reading' became a mantra
for the American New Critics,"[5] the first time that this was
restated in print was Vuilleumier's 1948 thesis (15)—nearly
two decades after the 1929 publication of Richards's *Practical
Criticism* (203). Strikingly, none of the New Critics themselves directly quoted Richards's turn of phrase as precedent,
though Brooks and Warren echoed its cadences: "really good
poetry will stand a great deal of close inspection" (199). Even
Richards himself never again spoke of "close reading" across
the remaining half century of his life. With the exception of a
passing reference in a 1973 festschrift for Richards, the attri-
bution wasn't circulated by scholars until the late 1980s. What
in retrospect looks like a slogan to us may have been more of

---

5. Todd Avery and Patrick Brantlinger, "Reading: 'Mind Hungers' Common and Uncommon," in *A Concise Companion to Modernism*, ed. David
Bradshaw (London: Wiley, 2002), 250.

a passing quip. Might Richards have been recalling Wilde's witticism "All bad poetry springs from genuine feeling" (162)?

1891:   Oscar Wilde, "The Critic as Artist, Part II," in *Intentions* (London: Heinemann & Balestier), 125–178.

1929:   I. A. Richards, *Practical Criticism: A Study of Literary Judgment* (London: Routledge & Kegan Paul).

1938:   Cleanth Brooks and Robert Penn Warren, *Understanding Poetry: An Anthology for College Students* (New York: Henry Holt).

1948:   Norman Etienne Vuilleumier, "A Preface to the Teaching of Poetry" (master's thesis, Boston University).

1973:   Elsie Duncan-Jones, "A Reading of Marvell's *The Unfortunate Lover*," in *I. A. Richards: Essays in his Honor*, ed. Reuben Brower, Helen Vendler,[6] and John Hollander (Oxford: Oxford University Press), 211–226.

1987:   Robert Miklitsch, "The Poppies of Practical Criticism: 'Rabbi, Read the Phases of This Difference'" [review essay on Helen Vendler's recent publications], *diacritics* 17.2 (Summer): 21–35.

6. Vendler, who studied with both Brower and Richards and was often lauded as "the closest of close readers" (Maureen N. McLane, "ROMANTICISM, or NOW: Learning to Read in Postmodern," *Modern Philology* 105.1 [August 2007]: 135), more than once expressed her vexation at the phrase "close reading," e.g., "The New Critics asked not for a 'close' reading, as it is nowadays referred to, but what I would call 'a writer's reading'" (Vendler, "Reading a Poem," in *Field Work: Sites in Literary and Cultural Studies*, ed. Marjorie Garber, Paul B. Franklin, and Rebecca L. Walkowitz [New York: Routledge, 1996], 129); and "We were said to practice something called 'close reading'—a rather absurd term, since what, if anything, would 'far reading' be? . . . *Intrinsic Criticism* seems to be closer to what we do than *close reading*" (Vendler, "Wallace Stevens: Hypotheses and Contradictions," *Representations* 81.1 [Winter 2003]: 100).

The well-wrought term

Before the consensus around the phrase "close reading" ultimately settled, competing alternatives included Ransom's "close criticism," Leavis's "close analytical study," Empson's "verbal analysis," and Wimsatt's "explication"/"explicitation," as well as "'exegesis,' 'interpretation,' 'elucidation,' 'exposition,' and 'paraphrase.'"[7] Even a single critic's vacillating terminology can be instructive, as evidenced across the career of Cleanth Brooks. None of his early publications deploys the precise wording "close reading," yet they all hover ambivalently around analogues such as "closer reading," "closer acquaintance," "thoughtful reading" (*Modern Poetry and the Tradition*, 23, 45, 110); "close analysis," "close inspection," "deeper level," "close scrutiny" (*Understanding Poetry*, 137, 199, 342, 674); and "closer reading," "adequate," or "exhaustive" readings (*The Well Wrought Urn*, 11, 193) It's almost as if Brooks were auditioning candidates for an apt catchphrase. He does include "close reading" in a 1949 foreword, if defensively: "though the text must provide the ultimate sanction for the meaning of the work," he begins, working up to his first variant on the idiom, "that does not mean that close textual reading is to be conceived of as a sort of verbal piddling" (xx); on the next page, he underscores: "The attempt to drive a wedge between close reading of the text and evaluation of the work seems to me confused and confusing" (xxi). In 1960

7. Fabian Gudas, "Explication," in *The New Princeton Encyclopedia of Poetry and Poetics*, ed. Alex Preminger and Terry V. F. Brogan (Princeton, NJ: Princeton University Press, 1993), 395.

Brooks experiments with extending the practice to prose fiction: "Does a novel like *Huckleberry Finn* require close reading?" he queries rhetorically (203), though even in this case he seems to prefer "intensive reading" (203, 204, 206, 213). In a 1961 essay, he resorts to placing "close reading" in scare quotes (70, 73), as if guardedly, as he does again in 1965, cautioning that "'close reading' can be mechanized and treated as though it were an end in itself" (xi). In 1971 a beleaguered tone emerges: "I sometimes feel that I too have been typed . . . as the rather myopic 'close reader,' the indefatigable exegete. In fact I am interested in a great many other things besides close reading" (231); here Brooks renews his 1947 plea for "adequate reading," as he would again in 1979 (600).

1939:   Cleanth Brooks, *Modern Poetry and the Tradition* (Charlotte: University of North Carolina Press).

1947:   Cleanth Brooks, *The Well Wrought Urn: Studies in the Structure of Poetry* (London: Dennis Dobson).

1949:   Cleanth Brooks, foreword to *Critiques and Essays in Criticism, 1920–1948*, ed. Robert W. Stallman[8] (New York: Ronald Press), xv–xxii.

1960:   Cleanth Brooks, "The Teaching of the Novel: *Huckleberry Finn*," in *Essays on the Teaching of English: Reports of the Yale Conferences on the Teaching of English*, ed. Edward J. Gordon and Edward S. Noyes, National Council of Teachers of English (New York: Appleton-Century-Crofts), 203–215.

8. Stallman appears to have been the first to mention "close readings" in *The New York Times*, "Letters to the Editor: New Criticism," May 29, 1955.

1961:   Cleanth Brooks, "The Criticism of Fiction: The Role
        of Close Analysis," in *The Critical Matrix*, ed. Paul R.
        Sullivan (Washington, DC: Georgetown University),
        67–90.

1965:   Cleanth Brooks, "A Retrospective Introduction," in *Modern Poetry & the Tradition* (Oxford: Oxford University
        Press), vii–xxvii.

1971:   Cleanth Brooks, *A Shaping Joy: Studies in the Writer's
        Craft* (London: Methuen).

1979:   Cleanth Brooks, "The New Criticism," *The Sewanee
        Review* 87.4 (Fall): 592–607.

The forest for the trees

The Tudor adage about being unable to "see the wood for
the trees"—dating at least as far back as More's 1533 *Confutacion of Tyndals Answere*—has served as a figure for the
limitations of close reading ever since 1947, when Schwartz
caricatured the New Critic as someone who "saw the trees,
the barks, the veins of the leaves, the roots, but he missed the
whole forest, such was his absorption. . . . the close criticism
of poetry does indeed lead to an inattention to the poem as
a whole" (708). In 1953 Van Wyck Brooks similarly complained about critical reading "so 'close' that one cannot see
the wood for the trees or the tree for the leaves" (20). The
saying perhaps gained an especial edge when Brooks and
Warren took their proverbial ax to Kilmer's "Trees" (1913),
"the most popular poem Harriet Monroe printed" in *Poetry*

magazine.[9] They bluntly snubbed this "very greatly admired" lyric as "a bad poem" (*Understanding Poetry*, 387). Brooks and Warren's hatchet job was widely anthologized,[10] yet it also engendered sharp rebuttals, starting with Fleece's 1951 attack on "close reading" itself, followed by many others.[11] The identification of close reading with missing-the-forest-for-the-"Trees" perhaps reached its apogee in 1967, when Nims satirized New Criticism via a *Dunciad*-like ("in closet close y-pent" [3.185]), mock-hyper-myopic analysis of Kilmer's poem. Moretti's trope of "trees" has revived the arboreal conceit, albeit in a remote context.

9. Joseph Parisi and Stephen Young, *Dear Editor: A History of Poetry in Letters: The First Fifty Years, 1912–1962* (New York: Norton, 2002), 8.

10. William H. Burton, Roland B. Kimball, and Richard L. Wing, eds., *Education for Effective Thinking: An Introductory Text* (New York: Appleton-Century-Crofts, 1960), 352; Myron Matlaw and James B. Stronks, eds., *Pro and Con* (Boston: Houghton Mifflin, 1960), 417; Robert B. Partlow, ed., *A Liberal Arts Reader* (Englewood Cliffs, NJ: Prentice-Hall, 1963), 388; Holley Gene Duffield, *Problems in Criticism of the Arts* (Scranton, PA: Chandler, 1968), 260; John Briggs and Richard Monaco, *Metaphor: The Logic of Poetry: A Handbook* (New York: Pace University Press, 1990), 240; Harvey S. Wiener, *Reading for the Disciplines: An Anthology for College Writers* (New York: McGraw-Hill, 1990), 335.

11. Marvin Fisher, "Another Hack at 'Trees,'" *College English* 19.2 (November 1957): 76; Barbara Garlitz, "Uprooting 'Trees,'" *College English* 23.4 (January 1962): 299–301; Blair G. Kenney, "Woodsman, Spare Those 'Trees'!," *College English* 25.6 (March 1964): 431–433; Paul Sawyer, "What Keeps 'Trees' Growing?" *CEA Critic* 33.1 (November 1970): 17–19; Michael Hancher, "Poems versus Trees: The Aesthetics of Monroe Beardsley," *The Journal of Aesthetics and Art Criticism* 31.2 (Winter 1972): 181–191; Jerome McGann, "The Alice Fallacy; or, Only God Can Make a Tree," in *Beauty and the Critic: Aesthetics in an Age of Cultural Studies* (Tuscaloosa: University of Alabama Press, 1997), 46–73; Naomi Levine, "Understanding Poetry Otherwise: New Criticism and Historical Poetics," *Literature Compass* 17.7 (July 21, 2020): 1–11.

1947: Delmore Schwartz, "The Noble View" [review of Mark Van Doren, *The Noble Voice*], *The Sewanee Review* 55.4 (October–December): 707–709.

1951: Jeffrey Fleece, "Further Notes on a 'Bad' Poem," *College English* 12.16 (March): 314–320.

1953: Van Wyck Brooks, *The Writer in America* (New York: Avon Books).

1967: John Frederick Nims, "The Greatest English Lyric?—A New Reading of Joe E. Skilmer's 'Therese,'" *Studies in Bibliography* 20: 1–14.

2007: Franco Moretti, *Graphs, Maps, Trees: Abstract Models for Literary History* (London: Verso).

When life gives you lemons . . .

In 1958 Gardner was the first critic to include "close reading" in a published title, which might imply that arguments *against* close reading belatedly flushed the term into the open, out from its latency. Wain's 1955 *Interpretations*, the essay collection reviewed by Gardner, had already generated sharp responses from others, including a perceptive evaluation by Hall: "The partisanship displayed for close reading has not been seen on this side of the Atlantic for at least twenty years . . . in fact, it has become sometimes a convention as blunt, stupid and mechanical as any habit of criticism has ever been" (45). Even more acerbic was Eliot, who dismissed the volume's method as "the lemon-squeezer school of criticism" (537). But Wain had the last word, titling the introduction to his revised 1972 edition "On the Squeezing of Lemons."

1955: John Wain, ed., *Interpretations: Essays on Twelve English Poems* (London: Routledge & Kegan Paul).

1956: T. S. Eliot, "The Frontiers of Criticism," *The Sewanee Review* 64.4 (October–December): 525–543.

1956: Donald Hall, review of Wain, *Interpretations*, paired with Larkin's *The Less Deceived*, *Shenandoah* 7.3 (Summer): 45–52.

1958: Stanley Gardner, "Close Reading Was Not Enough," *Essays in Criticism* 8.2 (April): 187–194.

1973: Bernard Bergonzi, "Critical Situations: From the Fifties to the Seventies" [review of John Wain's 1972 reissue of *Interpretations*], *Critical Quarterly* 15.1 (March): 59–73.

In weiter Ferne, so nah!

Weimann's initial foray into "close reading" is but a few pages—yet it's telling that by the 1960s continental European scholars had already begun to remark upon what they perceived to be a standard practice in Anglophone criticism. A 2023 Berlin conference called "Close Reading," organized by Philipp Felsch and Michael Gamper, resumes this tradition, as does a proposed University of Zurich compendium titled *Close Reading: Geschichte, Praktiken, Lektionen*, to be edited by Stefanie Heine, Rahel Villinger, and Sandro Zanetti.

1960: Robert Weimann, "'New Criticism' und bürgerliche Literaturwissenschaft: Geschichte und Kritik neuerer Strömungen," *Zeitschrift für Anglistik und Amerikanistik* 8: 29–74, 141–170.

1963: Johan Kuin, "Close reading en modern literaire kritiek," *Roeping* 38: 522–543.

1964: Willem Wilmink, *Syllabus close reading* (Amsterdam: Instituut voor Neerlandistiek).

1966: Lieve Scheer, *De poëtische werelde van Paul Snoek: Proeve van close-reading* (Brussels: Manteau).

1968: Herbert Grabes, "Close Reading und 'The Meaning of Meaning,'" *Anglia: Zeitschrift für Englische Philologie/ Journal of English Philology* 86: 321–338.

1970: W. Drop and J. W. Steenbeek, *Indringend lezen 1: "Close-reading" van poezie* (Groningen: Wolters-Noordhoff).

1973: *LWU: Literatur in Wissenschaft und Unterricht* [although this journal was founded at Kiel University (CAU) in 1968, when advertised in English in 1973, it added the explanatory subtitle "A Journal of Close Reading and Explication de Texte"].

Publishers take note

While Brooks and Warren's *Understanding Poetry* never refers to "close reading" across its four editions (1938–1976), a 1946 publisher's advertisement for the second edition did claim that until the arrival of their textbook, many teachers "could not teach the close reading of poetry," boasting that proof of the volume's "revolution is its influence on the authors of other textbooks. There are three other very good texts for the close reading of poetry now on the market."[12] Burtness et al.'s account of close reading is perfunctory (and Frohock's nonexistent), yet the advent of both classroom volumes in 1962 consolidates the term of art for pedagogical

12. *Saturday Review*, August 3, 1946, 2.

as well as marketing purposes. As evidence of the latter impulse, it's suggestive that Scott's 1968 sequel to his 1957 anthology *A Poet's Craft* was called *Close Readings*, being "intended to give students tools of the art of close reading comparable to those the critics themselves are using" (ix).

1962: Paul S. Burtness, Warren U. Ober, and William R. Seat, Jr., *The Close Reading of Factual Prose* (Evanston, IL: Row, Peterson).

1962: W. M. Frohock, *French Literature: An Approach through Close Reading* (Cambridge: Schoenhof's Foreign Books).

1968: A. F. Scott, *Close Readings: A Course in the Critical Appreciation of Poetry* (London: Heinemann).

Secondary-school pedagogy, part 1

Pressure to implement close reading at the secondary level led to the first wave of pedagogical handbooks (later swamped by a second wave, following the 2010 implementation of the Common Core State Standards Initiative—see below). Prior "hoped that [her] guide will help the teacher who has not previously had the opportunity to teach close reading of literature to direct the study of this novel" (1); Cline sought "to teach close reading of a story concentrating attention on setting, character, and theme" (2). "More than one generation of teachers learned from *Practical Criticism* how to teach close reading," according to Berthoff (196), yet Squire and Applebee's 1968 study worried that the "'bloodless' exercises in the close reading of a work" they observed "were completely removed from literature, life, or anything of meaning to students" (108). They attributed "the inadequate attention devoted to close reading in our nation's schools" to "heavy teaching load[s]" (110)—in fact, they concluded that "one of the most important findings emerging from this Study" was "the discovery that sustained attention to close reading may be possible only when teaching loads are reduced to permit adequate preparation" (111). Rosenblatt was less sanguine about what she perceived to be the dismal results of "several decades in which 'close reading' has been increasingly stressed in colleges and secondary schools" (64). From her perspective, "impersonal or objective criticism" fruitlessly "busied itself with exploitation of the techniques of 'close reading'" (281). By 1979, Parisi argued that the practice ought to move away from literature as its object, recommending instead that "student writing can be used to teach close reading" (62).

1966: Kathleen W. Prior, "Guide for Teaching the Novel *Island of the Blue Dolphins*, Grade 6" (San Diego: San Diego City Schools).

1968: Louise Rosenblatt, *Literature as Exploration*, revised ed. (New York: Noble & Noble).

1968: James R. Squire and Roger K. Applebee, *High School English Instruction Today: The National Study of High School English Programs* (Urbana, IL: National Council of Teachers of English).

1969: Jay Cline, "Voices in Literature, Language and Composition—2—Media Guide" (Boston: Ginn).

1979: Peter Parisi, "Close Reading, Creative Writing, and Cognitive Development," *College English* 41.1 (September): 57–67.

1980: Ann E. Berthoff, "I. A. Richards and the Philosophy of Rhetoric," *Rhetoric Society Quarterly* 10.4 (Autumn): 195–210.

SCOTT NEWSTOK

The institution of graduate study

By the late 1960s, titles foregrounding "close reading" began appearing in master's theses and dissertations about literary criticism as well as pedagogy; this would soon become a familiar (if formulaic) motif. Ducharme's thesis lamented that "despite the impact of the movement of close reading in higher education and educators' recent call for its practice in the high school, there is evidence that little close reading is done in secondary English classes," a regret he reiterated nearly a half century later: "one may see little evidence of close reading in schools because most teachers don't have the skills themselves and, consequently, cannot engage their students in it. Close reading is a skill that demands study and discipline" (48).

1967:   Ronald Everett Day, "A Close Reading of John Milton's *L'Allegro* and *Il Penseroso*" (undergraduate thesis, University of North Carolina).

1967:   Charles Henry MacFarland, "A Missal for Brooding-Sight: A Close Reading of Wallace Stevens's 'The Man with the Blue Guitar'" (undergraduate thesis, MIT).

1968:   Edward Robert Ducharme, "Close Reading and the Teaching of Poetry in English Education and in Secondary Schools" (EdD thesis, Teachers College, Columbia).

1968:   Ida Novak Myers, "On a Note of Grace: A Close Reading of Nelly Sachs' 'Beryll sieht in der nacht'" (master's thesis, UCLA).

1968:   James David Weiss, "The Relative Effects upon High School Students of Inductive and Programmed Instruction in the Close Reading of Poetry" (PhD thesis, New York University).

2014:   Edward R. Ducharme, "A Response to Peter and Cor-
        rine's Essay: New Criticism," *Style* 48.1 (Spring): 48–53.

"Nothing fails like success"[13]

A scholar once cautioned that "abuse of the 'new criticism's'
method of close reading and analysis of structures of meaning could lead to another form of pedantry."[14] This concern
was voiced in 1953; by 1960, Wellek acknowledged that this
risk had come to pass: "'Close reading' has led to pedantries and aberrations."[15] According to Webster, close reading
had established itself as "normal criticism" (adopting Kuhn's
concept of "normal science"). As Nemerov more jadedly observed in 1975: "the success of explicative criticism is exactly
its failure. . . . [T]he kind of 'close reading' I, along with
many of you, had been brought up to do [. . .] had run its
course. In a sense it seemed to have taught its lesson all too
successfully" (111–12). This sentiment about close reading's
diffusion was echoed in different registers by Culler ("we
are all New Critics now" [244]); Rubin ("it has become simply criticism" [683]); Heilman ("[t]here is a sense in which
Brooks was too popular" [328]); and Dickstein ("the New
Criticism died when it was universally assimilated" [63]).
Close reading has been routinely written off "as expired,
extinct, and belonging to another era—as dead rather than

13. "Public Affairs," *The Leader* 388 (August 29, 1857): 832.
14. Sholom Jacob Kahn, *Science and Aesthetic Judgment: A Study in Taine's
Critical Method* (New York: Columbia University Press, 1953), 184.
15. René Wellek, "Literary Theory, Criticism, and History," *The Sewanee
Review* 68 (Winter 1960): 9.

living on."[16] And yet, as Gerald Graff paraphrased Twain in his endorsement of *Close Reading: The Reader* (2002), "the alleged death of close reading at the hands of theory [. . .] [has] been greatly exaggerated."

1975:   Howard Nemerov, "Speaking Silence," *The Georgia Review* 29.4 (Winter): 865–881; reprinted in *Figures of Thought: Speculations on the Meaning of Poetry and Other Essays* (Boston: Godine, 1979).

1976:   Jonathan Culler, "Beyond Interpretation: The Prospects of Contemporary Criticism," *Comparative Literature* 28.3 (Summer): 244–256.

1979:   Grant Webster, "Close Reading as Normal Criticism," in *The Republic of Letters: A History of Postwar American Literary Opinion* (Baltimore, MD: Johns Hopkins University Press), 95–102.

1980:   Louis D. Rubin, Jr., "Tory Formalists, New York Intellectuals, and the New Historical Science of Criticism," *The Sewanee Review* 88.4 (Fall): 674–683.

1983:   Robert B. Heilman, "Cleanth Brooks and *The Well Wrought Urn*," *The Sewanee Review* 91.2 (Spring): 322–334.

2005:   Morris Dickstein, "The Rise and Fall of 'Practical' Criticism: From I. A. Richards to Barthes and Derrida," *Theory's Empire: An Anthology of Dissent*, ed. Daphne Patai and Will Corral (New York: Columbia University Press), 60–77.

16. Sara Guyer, *Reading with John Clare: Biopoetics, Sovereignty, Romanticism* (New York: Fordham University Press, 2015), 7.

2018:   William E. Cain, "British and American New Criticism,"
        in *A Companion to Literary Theory*, ed. David H. Richter
        (London: Wiley-Blackwell), 11–23.

"In theory, there is no difference between theory and practice; but in practice, there is"[17]

In the mid-1960s de Man observed that "New Criticism has turned into the fruitful and didactically effective discipline of close reading," and yet was "unable itself to lead to larger undertakings."[18] More portentously, Hartman asserted that "the dominion of Exegesis is great: she is our Whore of Babylon, sitting robed in Academic black on the great dragon of Criticism, and dispensing a repetitive and soporific balm from her pedantic cup."[19] For decades, High Theory's proponents have maintained that it was an elaboration of (an exhausted) close reading, which was "just not close enough."[20] While others (e.g., Poirier or Ricks) have disputed the affiliation, "close reading," averred one critic, "occupies

17. Often misattributed to Yogi Berra; first cited by Walter J. Cavitch, *Pascal: An Introduction to the Art and Science of Programming* (Redwood City, CA: Benjamin-Cummings, 1984), 129.

18. "Spacecritics," *Partisan Review* 31.4 (Fall 1964): 640.

19. "Beyond Formalism," *MLN* 81.5 (December 1966): 556.

20. David Kaufer and Gary Waller, "To Write Is to Read Is to Write, Right?," in *Writing and Reading Differently: Deconstruction and the Teaching of Composition and Literature*, ed. G. Douglas Atkins and Michael L. Johnson (Lawrence: University of Kansas Press, 1985), 86.

a motherhood position in critical method,"[21] authorizing
the work of scholars as varied as Gates, Greenblatt,[22] Said,
Sedgwick, and Spivak; Derrida himself held that "political,
ethical and juridical responsibility requires a task of infinite
close reading."[23] In "its disseminated state, theory now . . . often arrives in tandem with close readings of literary texts."[24]

1984:   Henry Louis Gates, Jr. "Criticism in the Jungle," in *Black
        Literature and Literary Theory*, ed. Henry Louis Gates,
        Jr. (London: Methuen), 1–24.

1985:   Barbara Johnson, "Teaching Deconstructively," in
        *Writing and Reading Differently: Deconstruction and the
        Teaching of Composition and Literature*, ed. G. Douglas
        Atkins and Michael L. Johnson (Lawrence: University
        Press of Kansas), 140–48.

1988:   Stephen Greenblatt, "The Circulation of Social Energy,"
        in *Shakespearean Negotiations* (Berkeley: University of
        California Press), 1–20.

21. J. M. Q. Davies, *Bridging the Gap: Literary Theory in the Classroom*
(West Cornwall, CT: Locust Hill Press, 1994), 171.

22. According to Donald Pease, New Historicists "turn one of the preroga-
tives of a close reader into an historical agency. Like the close reader . . . they
remake American history by making it seem in need of a field made up of close
readings." "New Americanists: Revisionist Interventions into the Canon,"
boundary 2 17.1 (Spring 1990): 16.

23. Jacques Derrida, "Hospitality, Justice and Responsibility: A Dialogue,"
in *Questioning Ethics: Contemporary Debates in Philosophy*, ed. Richard Kear-
ney and Mark Dooley (London: Routledge, 1998), 57.

24. Judith Butler, John Guillory, and Kendall Thomas, "Preface," in *What's
Left of Theory? New Work on the Politics of Literary Theory*, ed. Judith Butler,
John Guillory, and Kendall Thomas (New York: Routledge, 2000), xi.

1992: Richard Poirier, "Reading Pragmatically," in *Poetry and Pragmatism* (Cambridge, MA: Harvard University Press), 171–193.

1996: Christopher Ricks, "Literary Principles as Against Theory," in *Essays in Appreciation* (Oxford: Oxford University Press), 311–332.

1997: Eve Kosofsky Sedgwick, "Paranoid Reading and Reparative Reading; or, You're So Paranoid, You Probably Think This Introduction Is about You," in *Novel Gazing: Queer Readings in Fiction*, ed. Eve Kosofsky Sedgwick (Durham, NC: Duke University Press), 1–37.

2000: Julian Wolfreys, *Readings: Acts of Close Reading in Literary Theory* (Edinburgh: Edinburgh University Press).

2004: Edward W. Said, "The Return to Philology," in *Humanism and Democratic Criticism* (New York: Columbia University Press), 57–84.

2005: Eric Hayot, "'The Slightness of My Endeavor': An Interview with Gayatri Chakravorty Spivak," *Comparative Literature* 57.3 (Summer): 256–272.

To infinity . . . and beyond!

One senses a mounting impatience with close reading in the 1990s, with scholars "scouring the horizon beyond close reading" for something to supersede it (Wolff 52). The exasperation's palpable in titles such as "Against Close Reading" (Rabinowitz), "Textual Harassment" (Armstrong), "On the Impossibility of Close Reading" (Elkins), "Beyond the Current Impasse in Literary Studies" (Poovey), and "Should College English Be Close Reading?" (Bialostosky). While "close reading came to be represented . . . as the whipping boy of various leftist agendas,"[25] Brown submits that "we'd do better . . . to see 'close reading' as a practice that can be used in either conservative or progressive ways; it isn't ontologically incorrect," nor does it represent "an inherent politics."[26] Nonetheless, as if in response to pent-up demand, alternative nomenclature began to proliferate once more in the early 2000s, just as it had before the 1950s settlement; new modifiers of "reading" included: *actual, affective, analytical, assigned, attentive, calibrated, close but not deep, closer, cognitive, compulsive, critical, deep, denaturalized, denotative, descriptive, dialectical, digital, distant, distracted, ecological, electronic, embodied, engaged, enumerative, extensive, flat, formal, hyper, immersive, inattentive, intensive, interfaced, just, large, lay, literal, literary, lyric, machine, medium-close, mere, micro, middle, middle-distant, nostalgic, not, object-oriented, outraged, paranoid, patient, pleasure, plural, postcritical, professional, proximate, reflective, reparative, repeat, responsible, restorative, serial, slow, surface, suspicious, symptomatic, technical, tedious, thin, thick, too-close, tracked, translated, uncritical, wakeful* . . . "the rest were long to tell."[27] As Battersby surmises, "The modesty of the modifiers critics use to describe their approaches" might be "a telling indication that such practices are characterized more by the critical

25. Cecily Devereux, "'A Kind of Dual Attentiveness': Close Reading after the New Criticism," in *Rereading the New Criticism*, ed. Miranda B. Hickman and John D. McIntyre (Columbus: Ohio State University Press, 2012), 219.

26. Matthew P. Brown, "How Is Cultural Studies Anyway? Evidence, Discipline, and the Iconographical Impulse," *The Journal of the Midwest Modern Language Association* 34.3 (Autumn 2001): 61, 66.

27. John Milton, *Paradise Lost* (1.506; 12.260–61).

manoeuvres they refuse to perform than any novel strategies for the interpretation of texts."[28]

1991: Heather Murray, "Close Reading, Closed Writing," *College English* 53.2 (February): 195–208.

1992: Peter J. Rabinowitz, "Against Close Reading," in *Pedagogy Is Politics: Literary Theory and Critical Teaching*, ed. Marina-Regina Kecht (Urbana: University of Illinois Press), 230–244.

1994: Stephen Booth, "Close Reading without Readings," in *Shakespeare Reread: The Texts in New Contexts*, ed. Russ McDonald (Ithaca, NY: Cornell University Press), 42–55.

1995: Isobel Armstrong, "Textual Harassment: The Ideology of Close Reading, or How Close is Close?" *Textual Practice* 9.3 (Winter): 401–420.

1996: James Elkins, "On the Impossibility of Close Reading: The Case of Alexander Marshack," *Current Anthropology* 37.2 (April): 185–226.

1999: Mary Poovey, "Beyond the Current Impasse in Literary Studies," *American Literary History* 11.2 (Summer): 354–377.

2006: Don Bialostosky, "Should College English Be Close Reading?" *College English* 69.2 (November): 111–116.

2007: G. Gabrielle Starr, "Poetic Subjects and Grecian Urns: Close Reading and the Tools of Cognitive Science," *Modern Philology* 105.1 (August): 48–61.

28. "Reading by Example: Disciplinary History," in *The Work of Reading: Literary Criticism in the 21st Century*, ed. Anirudh Sridhar, Mir Ali Hosseini, and Derek Attridge (Cham, Switz.: Palgrave Macmillan, 2021), 97 n. 27.

2009: Stephen Best and Sharon Marcus, "Surface Reading: An Introduction," *Representations* 108.1 (Fall): 1–21.

2009: Maryanne Wolf and Mirit Barzillai, "The Importance of Deep Reading," *Educational Leadership* 66.6 (March): 32–37.

2013: Heather Love, "Close Reading and Thin Description," *Public Culture* 25.3 (Fall): 401–434.

2019: Tristram Wolff, "That's Close Enough: The Unfinished History of Emotivism in Close Reading," *PMLA* 134.1 (January): 51–65.

2021: Helena Feder, "Introduction: The Unbearable Closeness of Reading," in *Close Reading the Anthropocene*, ed. Helena Feder (Abingdon, UK: Routledge), 1–14.

"To live and to understand fully, we need not only proximity but also distance"[29]

In the wake of two polemical essays from 2000, Moretti was frequently credited with coining the spatial trope of "distant reading"—what Arac called "new formalism without close reading."[30] As many have observed, the *practice* (of quantitative textual analysis) preceded Moretti, whether you point to Burrows's 1987 computational study of Austen, Miles's 1940s hand-tabulated phrasal forms, Rickert's

29. Walter J. Ong, SJ, "Writing Is a Technology That Restructures Thought," in *The Written Word: Literacy in Transition*, ed. Gerd Baumann (Oxford: Oxford University Press, 1986), 32.

30. Jonathan Arac, "Anglo-Globalism?" *New Left Review* n.s. 16 (2002): 41.

1927 statistical analyses of style, or an even earlier "range of nineteenth-century experiments" (Underwood). Less well-known is that the *phrase* ("distant reading") likewise precedes Moretti—although, before him, it was more often deployed in derision than in praise, as when one scholar in 1974 objected to the "imprecision" of the phrase "close reading . . . by asking what its apparent opposite, distant reading, could possibly be."[31] Another scoffed in 1989: "I do not think that 'close reading' is a very helpful description of the activity I am trying to describe—has one ever heard of 'distant reading'"?[32] Yet while he originated neither the phrase nor the practice, Moretti did give "distant reading" a kind of escape velocity—launching it into public discourse (and social media), where it could be sloganized as a ready antonym to (purportedly) antiquated scholarly routines. In a prefatory note to the 2013 book version of "Conjectures," Moretti reflects on the unexpected trajectory of his bon mot:

> *That fatal formula had been a late addition to the paper, where it was initially specified, in an allusion to the basic procedure of quantitative history, by the words "serial reading." Then, somehow, "serial" disappeared, and "distant" remained. Partly, it was meant as a joke; a moment of relief in a rather relentless argument. But no one seems to have taken it as a joke, and they were probably right.* (44)

31. Alan Kennedy, *The Protean Self: Dramatic Action in Contemporary Fiction* (London: Macmillan, 1974), 1.

32. T. A. Birrell, "English as a Foreign Literature and the Decline of Philology," *English Studies* 70.6 (1989): 581–586.

1927: Edith Rickert, *New Methods for the Study of Literature* (Chicago: University of Chicago Press).

1987: J. F. Burrows, *Computation into Criticism: A Study of Jane Austen's Novels and an Experiment in Method* (Oxford: Clarendon Press).

2000: Franco Moretti, "Conjectures on World Literature," *New Left Review* (January–February): 54–68.

2000: Franco Moretti, "The Slaughterhouse of Literature," *MLQ: Modern Language Quarterly* 61.1 (March): 207–227.

2005: Peter Middleton, *Distant Reading: Performance, Readership, and Consumption in Contemporary Poetry* (Tuscaloosa: University of Alabama Press).

2012: Matthew Wilkens, "Canons, Close Reading, and the Evolution of Method," in *Debates in the Digital Humanities*, ed. Matthew Gold (Minneapolis: University of Minnesota Press), 249–258.

2013: Matthew Jockers, *Macroanalysis: Digital Methods and Literary History* (Urbana: University of Illinois Press).

2013: Franco Moretti, *Distant Reading* (London: Verso).

2014: Jessica Pressman, "Close Reading: Marshall McLuhan, From Modernism to Media Studies," in *Digital Modernism: Making It New in New Media* (Oxford: Oxford University Press), 28–55.

2015: Yohei Igarashi, "Statistical Analysis at the Birth of Close Reading," *New Literary History* 46.3 (June): 485–504.

2016: Adam Hammond, Julian Brooke, and Graeme Hirst, "Modeling Modernist Dialogism: Close Reading with Big Data," in *Reading Modernism with Machines: Digital Humanities and Modernist Literature*, ed. Shawna Ross and James O'Sullivan (London: Palgrave), 49–77.

2016: Andrew Kopec, "The Digital Humanities, Inc.: Literary Criticism and the Fate of a Profession," *PMLA* 131.2 (March): 324–339.

2016: Hoyt Long and Richard Jean So, "Literary Pattern Recognition: Modernism between Close Reading and Machine Learning," *Critical Inquiry* 42.2 (Winter): 235–267.

2017: Katherine Bode, "The Equivalence of 'Close' and 'Distant' Reading; or, Toward a New Object for Data-Rich Literary History." *Modern Language Quarterly* 78.1 (March): 77–106.

2017: Jay Jin, "Problems of Scale in 'Close' and 'Distant' Reading," *Philological Quarterly* 96.1 (Winter): 105–129.

2017: Ted Underwood, "A Genealogy of Distant Reading," *Digital Humanities Quarterly* 11.2, http://www.digitalhumanities.org/dhq/vol/11/2/000317/000317.html.

2018: Rachel Sagner Buurma and Laura Heffernan, "Search and Replace: Josephine Miles and the Origins of Distant Reading," *Modernism/modernity* 3.1 (April), https://modernismmodernity.org/forums/posts/search-and-replace.

2019: Martin Paul Eve, *Close Reading with Computers: Textual Scholarship, Computational Formalism, and David Mitchell's "Cloud Atlas"* (Stanford, CA: Stanford University Press).

2022: Kiriloff Gabi, "Computation as Context: New Approaches to the Close/Distant Reading Debate," *College Literature* 49.1 (Winter): 1–25.

2023: Colette Gordon, "Reading Literature In/Against the Digital Age: Shallow Assumptions, Deep Problems, Expectant Pedagogies," in *Convergence: The International Journal of Research into New Media Technologies* (January): 28–46.

Secondary-school pedagogy, part 2:
The Common Core

It's no exaggeration to assert that the Common Core State Standards Initiative has done more to disseminate the notion of "close reading" in schools than any other single event, person, or institution. In but a few years, this initiative reenshrined close reading in primary and secondary education across the United States; whether that's been a beneficial development remains a matter of fervent contention. Intriguingly, the initial 2010 CCSS guidance for English Language Arts & Literacy didn't require "close reading" per se, but rather called for students to "undertake the **close**, attentive **reading** that is at the heart of understanding and enjoying complex works of literature" (3); likewise, the CCSS "Anchor Standard 1 in Reading" expected students to "**Read closely** to determine what the text says explicitly and to make logical inferences from it; cite specific textual evidence when writing or speaking to support conclusions drawn from the text" (10). Within the context of the CCSS, the precise term "close reading" seems to have first appeared in 2011 workshops led by Coleman, the Standards' soi-disant "architect" (and soon to become president of the College Board); shortly thereafter, "close reading" was formally incorporated in the 2012 Publisher's Criteria, co-written by Coleman and Pimentel.[33] Since

33. The Criteria encourage "close, sustained reading of complex text . . . focus[ing] on what lies within the four corners of a text" (4). Modeling his own guidance, in 2013 Coleman counseled teachers to minimize the preliminary presentation of the context of "Letter from Birmingham Jail," a strategy

this bigram hadn't previously been employed by most precollegiate educators, its novelty provoked considerable anxiety among the teaching professoriate about how to implement the standards. Sensing an opportunity, educational presses and consultants hastened to produce handouts, textbooks, lesson plans, and associated pedagogical materials, leading to the remarkable post-2010 surge in publications about "close reading" (though rarely did these take into account the long pre-CCSS history of the practice). Many veteran teachers were skeptical about what they perceived to be the latest abstract buzzword; some vehemently opposed the apparent incoherence of expecting close reading to somehow come before basic comprehension at the primary level. Moreover, this mode of "close reading" has, in its reduced application, fixated classroom pedagogy on radically decontextualized excerpts. Indeed, Hirsch—certainly no stranger to "validity in interpretation"!—has contended that encouraging close reading "as a mode of actual reading of texts or the testing of reading comprehension is a mistake unjustified by credible research" (110).

---

that the radically embedded nature of King's epistle itself would seem to contradict; https://vimeo.com/27056255. More notoriously, in a 2011 presentation Coleman disparaged the proclivity to assign "personal writing" in secondary education: "As you grow up in this world, you realize that people really don't give a shit about what you feel or what you think." "Bringing the Common Core to Life," New York State Education Department conference (April 28, 2011). https://www.youtube.com/watch?app=desktop&v=DBTRmBJWICY; transcript: http://my-ecoach.com/online/resources/12842/Bringing_the_Common_Core_to_Life.pdf.

2010:   "Common Core Standards for English Language
        Arts & Literacy in History/Social Studies, Science,
        and Technical Subjects," *Common Core State Standards
        Initiative* (June 2), https://www.thecorestandards.org/
        wp-content/uploads/ELA_Standards1.pdf.

2010:   Heather Horn, "Stop Close Reading," *The Atlantic* (July 1),
        https://www.theatlantic.com/projects/ideas-2010/
        archive/2010/07/stop-close-reading/59005/.

2012:   Kylene Beers and Robert E. Probst, *Notice & Note:
        Strategies for Close Reading* (Portsmouth, NH:
        Heinemann).

2012:   Sheila Brown and Lee Kappes, "Implementing the
        Common Core State Standards: A Primer on 'Close
        Reading of Text,'" *Aspen Institute* (October 4),
        https://www.aspeninstitute.org/wp-content/uploads/
        2012/10/Implementing-the-Common-Core-State
        -Standards.pdf.

2012:   David Coleman and Susan Pimentel, "Revised Pub-
        lishers' Criteria for the Common Core State Standards
        in English Language Arts and Literacy, Grades 3–12"
        (April 4), https://hcommons.org/app/uploads/sites/
        1002005/2023/06/Coleman-and-Pimentel-Revised
        -Publishers-Criteria-for-the-Common-Core-S-1.pdf.

2012:   PARCC [Partnership for Assessment of Readiness for
        College and Careers], MODEL CONTENT FRAME-
        WORKS ENGLISH LANGUAGE ARTS/LITERACY,
        GRADES 3–11, Version 2.0 (August), https://files.eric.ed
        .gov/fulltext/ED582077.pdf.

2013:   Kathleen A. Hinchman and David W. Moore,
        "Close Reading: A Cautionary Interpretation,"
        Journal of Adolescent & Adult Literacy 56.6 (March):
        441–450.

2013: Christopher Lehman and Kate Roberts, *Falling in Love with Close Reading: Lessons for Analyzing Texts—and Life* (Portsmouth, NH: Heinemann).

2015: "Learning to Read," special issue of *PMLA* 130.3 (May 2015) [includes a cluster of essays on the Common Core, some of which address close reading].

2016: E. D. Hirsch, *Why Knowledge Matters: Rescuing Our Children from Failed Educational Theories* (Cambridge, MA: Harvard Education Press).

2017: Amy Koehler Catterson and P. David Pearson, "A Close Reading of Close Reading: What Does the Research Tell Us about How to Promote the Thoughtful Interrogation of Text?," in *Adolescent Literacies: A Handbook of Practice-Based Research*, ed. Kathleen A. Hinchman and Deborah A. Appleman (New York: Guilford Press), 457–475.

2019: Meaghan Brewer, "The Closer the Better? The Perils of an Exclusive Focus on Close Reading," *Journal of Adolescent and Adult Literacy* 62.6 (May–June): 635–642.

2019: Jodi G. Welsch, Jennifer Jones Powell, and Valerie J. Robnolt, "Getting to the Core of Close Reading: What Do We Really Know and What Remains to be Seen?," *Reading Psychology* 40.1 (February): 95–116.

2019: Natalie Wexler, *The Knowledge Gap: The Hidden Cause of America's Broken Education System—and How to Fix It* (New York: Avery).

2022: Jaclyn Carter, Michael Tavel Clarke, Faye Halpern, Derritt Mason, Jessica Nicol, and Morgan Vanek, "Too Close for Context: Where Students Get Stuck When Close Reading," *Pedagogy* 22.3 (October): 349–371.

SCOTT NEWSTOK

"They must retrench; that did not admit of a doubt"[34]

Animated in part by the emergence of "distant reading" (as well as the above-noted litany of alternative reading practices), conferences, special issues, handbooks, anthologies, and edited collections have sought to articulate rationales behind "the return of close reading with a difference."[35]

2003: Andrew DuBois, "Close Reading: An Introduction," in *Close Reading: The Reader*, ed. Frank Lentricchia and Andrew DuBois (Durham, NC: Duke University Press), 1–40.

2006: Francine Prose, "Close Reading: Learning to Write by Learning to Read," *The Atlantic* (August).

2007: Jane Gallop, "The Historicization of Literary Studies and the Fate of Close Reading," *Profession*: 181–186.

2009: Barry Brummett, *Techniques of Close Reading* (Thousand Oaks, CA: SAGE).

2009: "Close Reading: A Preface," *SubStance* 38.2: 3–7.

2009: Roland Greene, "Close Reading Transformed: The New Criticism and the World," in *A Touch More Rare: Harry Berger, Jr., and the Arts of Interpretation*, ed. Nina Levine and David Lee Miller (New York: Fordham University Press), 115–124.

34. Jane Austen, *Persuasion* (London: John Murray, 1817), 23.
35. Mieke Bal, "Close-Ups and Mirrors: The Return of Close Reading with a Difference," in *The Practice of Cultural Analysis: Exposing Interdisciplinary Interpretation* (Stanford, CA: Stanford University Press, 1999), 137.

2010: Jonathan Culler, "The Closeness of Close Reading," *ADE Bulletin* 149: 20–25.

2010: John Guillory, "Close Reading: Prologue and Epilogue," *ADE Bulletin* 149: 8–14.

2010: N. Katherine Hayles, "How We Read: Close, Hyper, Machine," *ADE Bulletin* 150: 62–79.

2011: Andrew Goldstone, "Close Reading as Genre," *Stanford Arcade*, https://shc.stanford.edu/arcade/interventions/close-reading-genre.

2015: Paula M. Moya, *The Social Imperative: Race, Close Reading, and Contemporary Literary Criticism* (Stanford, CA: Stanford University Press).

2016: Annette Federico, *Engagements with Close Reading* (Abingdon, UK: Routledge).

2019: David Greenham, *Close Reading: The Basics* (Abingdon, UK: Routledge).

2021: Paul Cobley and Johan Siebers, "Close Reading and Distance: Between Invariance and a Rhetoric of Embodiment," *Language Sciences* 84 (March).

2023: Jonathan Kramnick, "Close Reading," in *Criticism and Truth: On Method in Literary Studies* (Chicago: University of Chicago Press), 31–50.

2024: Jane Gallop, Eric Hayot, Ellen McCallum, and Gary Weissman, eds., forum, "The Ethics of Close Reading?," *symplokē* 32.1–2 (December).

2025: Marion Thain and Ewan Jones, eds., *Close Reading as Attentional Practice* (Edinburgh: Edinburgh University Press).

2025: Dan Sinykin and Johanna Winant, eds., *Close Reading for the Twenty-First Century* (Princeton, NJ: Princeton University Press).

"It would of course be a long though very useful job to write a full history of close reading"[36]

The desire to articulate close reading's present comes twinned with the probing of its past—yet "Why did it take so long to start writing the history of close reading?"[37] Rovee speculates that

> resurgent interest in the origins of close reading is not a
> sign that close reading has gone missing in itself. It ob-
> viously has not. Rather, it is a sign of close reading's
> imaginary relation to something that *has* gone missing:
> a confidence—underwritten by political culture and en-
> abled by asynchronous funding streams, and thus possible
> only in the fleeting and contradictory circumstances of the
> postwar academy—that what happens in college literature
> classrooms and in the pages of academic periodicals is val-
> ued by the culture at large. (4)

1996:   Chris Baldick, "Close Reading and the Rise of New
        Criticism," in *Criticism and Literary Theory, 1890 to the
        Present* (London: Longman), 78–85.

36. John Bowen, "Post-Structuralism, Pedagogy, Politics: The American Connection," in *Jean-François Lyotard, Critical Evaluations in Cultural Theory*, vol. 3, *Ethics*, ed. Victor E. Taylor and Gregg Lambert (London: Routledge, 2006), 47.

37. Angus Connell Brown, "Cultural Studies and Close Reading," *PMLA* 132.5 (October 2017): 1187.

2011: Joshua Gang, "Behaviorism and the Beginnings of Close Reading," *ELH* 78.1 (Spring): 1–25.

2012: David Ciccoricco, "The Materialities of Close Reading: 1942, 1959, 2009," *Digital Humanities Quarterly* 6.1, https://www.digitalhumanities.org/dhqdev/vol/6/1/ 000113/000113.html.

2012: Cecily Devereux, "'A Kind of Dual Attentiveness': Close Reading after the New Criticism," in *Rereading the New Criticism*, ed. Miranda B. Hickman and John D. McIntyre (Columbus: Ohio State University Press), 218–230.

2012: Esther Yu, "From Judgment to Interpretation: Eighteenth-Century Critics of Milton's *Paradise Lost*," *Milton Studies* 53: 181–208.

2013: Donald J. Childs, *The Birth of the New Criticism: Conflict and Conciliation in the Early Work of William Empson, I. A. Richards, Laura Riding, and Robert Graves* (Montreal: McGill-Queen's University Press).

2013: Joseph North, "What's 'New Critical' about 'Close Reading'? I. A. Richards and His New Critical Reception," *New Literary History* 44.1 (Winter): 141–157.

2014: Angus Connell Brown, "Between Lines: Close Reading, Quotation, and Critical Style from Practical Criticism to Queer Theory" (PhD thesis, Oxford University).

2015: Helen Thaventhiran, *Radical Empiricists: Five Modernist Close Readers* (Oxford: Oxford University Press).

2016: Barbara Herrnstein Smith, "What Was 'Close Reading'? A Century of Method in Literary Studies," *the minnesota review* 87: 57–75.

2019: Elizabeth Pender, "Exemplarity and Quotation: Ezra Pound's *How to Read*, Modernist Criticism, and the Limits of Close Reading," *Critical Quarterly* 61.1 (May): 67–81.

2020: Kent Cartwright, "Close Reading and New Criticism," in *The Arden Research Handbook of Contemporary Shakespeare Criticism*, ed. Evelyn Gajowski (London: Bloomsbury), 21–37.

2020: David James, ed., *Modernism and Close Reading* (Oxford: Oxford University Press).

2020: Andrew Rejan, "Re-Opening Close Reading: Literature Education and Literary Experience" (PhD thesis, Columbia University).

2022: Mark Byron, "Close Reading," *Oxford Encyclopedia of Literary Theory*, ed. John Frow (Oxford: Oxford University Press), 1637–1661.

2022: Alejandro Cathey-Cevallos, "Examining Romanticism: English Studies and the Emergence of Close Reading, 1904–1930" (PhD thesis, University of Edinburgh).

2024: Christopher Rovee, *New Critical Nostalgia: Romantic Lyric and the Crisis of Academic Life* (New York: Fordham University Press).

2024: Yael Segalovitz, *How Close Reading Made Us: The Transnational Legacies of New Criticism* (Albany: SUNY Press).

2025: Debra Gettelman, Audrey Jaffe, and Mary Ann O'Farrell, eds., *The Time of Close Reading: Victorian Fiction's Presents* (forthcoming).

2025: Mun-Hou Lo, ed., *Close Reading and Its Alternatives: An Essential Reader* (Routledge).

ACKNOWLEDGMENTS

I have been writing on the subject of close reading for many years, in work both published and unpublished on I. A. Richards. Some of this work was presented in lectures given at Johns Hopkins, Yale, Ohio State, NYU, Williams College, and the MLA annual conference. I presented an early version of the argument in the present book to a media studies seminar at Yale University in January of 2017. I am grateful to the media studies group for giving me the opportunity to explore the possibility of approaching close reading as a cultural technique. Since that time, I have delivered lectures on close reading at Harvard, Brown, Yonsei University (South Korea), Southern Methodist University, and Concordia University. I am grateful to these audiences for their invaluable responses. The final version of this short book was composed at the same time that I was seeing a much longer parallel project, *Professing Criticism: Essays on the Organization of Literary Study*, through to publication, also with the University of Chicago Press. I have discussed subjects related to close reading with many of the same colleagues and friends acknowledged in the earlier book. Among them, I owe the greatest long-standing debt to David Laurence, with whom I have discussed the teaching of reading for many decades. I am also grateful, as always, to Alan Thomas of the University of Chicago Press, who recognized the potential of what was an impossibly long essay to stand alone as a small book.

I owe my greatest debt to the conversation and research of Scott Newstok, who has provided both the bibliography appended to this book and an online archive documenting what scholars have written about close reading from the prehistory of our discipline to the present. I have employed the archive extensively to explore hypotheses, as well as to avoid errors of fact and nuance. This book would not have been possible without recourse to the archive, nor without recourse to the shrewd observations of Newstok on his research and my own. He has been a collaborator on this project in a measure difficult fully to convey. I must, of course, in the convention of scholarly acknowledgment, claim responsibility for whatever errors have survived.

INDEX